PRELUDE TO EMPIRE:

Portugal Overseas
Before Henry the Navigator

By

BAILEY W. DIFFIE

A Bison Book Original

University of Nebraska Press: 1960

First printing: December, 1960
Second printing: December, 1963
Third printing: January, 1967
Fourth printing: March, 1969
Fifth printing: May, 1972

LITHOPRINTED IN THE UNITED STATES OF AMERICA BY
CUSHING - MALLOY, INC., ANN ARBOR, MICHIGAN, 1972

TO MY SON WHITFIELD

PREFACE

Now you know why the caravel was such a remarkable vessel. She had to be. And the caravel . . . was the result of the Infante D. Henrique's happy marriage of mathematical learning to practical seamanship . . . and constant experimentation in Portuguese and Andalusian shipyards.

Andalusian as well as Portuguese, I say; for the Niebla region where Columbus fitted out borders on Portugal.

Samuel Eliot Morison,
Admiral of the Ocean Sea,
I, xl-xli

This small book deals with a period ending when the work of Henry the Navigator began. It is designed for the general reader, the college student, and also the specialist, inasmuch as it utilizes some archival study as well as the principal printed works. Its objective is to show the importance of Portuguese overseas experience before 1415 to the later period of the Great Discoveries. Its thesis, briefly stated, is that without a Henry the Navigator there would have been no Atlantic discoveries, and without the preceding centuries of commerce and fishing, there would have been no Navigator. Henry's name is but a convenient substitute for the thousands of men whose work he epitomizes, but it is the most important name among them.

This does not purport to be a definitive work — whatever that term may mean. No attempt has been made to be exhaustive. If compilation of data had been the purpose, there is material enough to fill a hundred times the present number of pages, even though the data are so scarce that hardly a single important point can be verified beyond dispute. Furthermore, a definitive work would have required the re-examination of the Latin and

Portuguese manuscripts which served as the texts for the printed documents herein cited. To believe that such a task is invariably necessary presupposes that the only worthwhile scholarship is the editing of documents, with every editor discrediting the work of his predecessors. Such was not the task I undertook. Moreover, a catalogue of materials would still leave the reader short of enough facts to lead to irrefutable conclusions.

There are no great new revelations herein. Historians have long found the subject matter interesting, and much has been written on it even in English, much more in Portuguese, French, Italian, and German. The interested reader can easily find additional works. For example, Professor P. E. Russell of Oxford has adequately, eruditely, and interestingly covered the periods of Edward III and Richard II of England — in 600 pages. For those who read Portuguese there is the twelve-volume work of Gama Barros.

What excuse can I offer for this book? In this age when there seem to be more people writing than reading, every author owes his potential reader an explanation. I shall answer my own question by posing one to the reader, whether specialist or non-specialist. Do you know of another book, in any language, of convenient size that attempts the task assumed in these few pages? Many tell much more, many tell a portion of the story, but none exactly and briefly what is written here.

Perhaps a few additional words will help the reader in using the book. All the important works that gave a positive result are cited in the notes. Every researcher knows that the principal portion of his time is spent in following false trails to negative results. While there is always something that even the most zealous searcher does not find, I believe that the books and articles hereafter cited give substantially the whole story. Citations, however, do not pinpoint the exact page and line. Had such a procedure been followed, there would have been several hundred notes and needless repetition of the published documents from which the bulk of the story has been drawn. Usually the notes group several works which bear on the general subject matter.

A short-title catalogue here takes the place of a bibliography. The full title may be found by turning to the chapter and foot-note number indicated. A brief-title bibliography (page 113) takes the place of a more extensive bibliography. The full title and bibliographical information are found in the note where a work is first cited. For example, the full information concerning Almeida, *História de Portugal,* as it is listed on page 113, is found in the Notes, Chapter I, footnote 1 (page 91).

The proper names of persons outside the Iberian Peninsula are usually given in the English forms. Peninsular names are given in the form by which the persons were known. Thus, João I of Portugal is easily differentiated from Juan I of Castile, whereas if both were called John much confusion would arise. Afonso and Henrique are Portuguese; Alfonso and Enrique, Spanish. Two exceptions have been made: Henry of Burgundy and Henry the Navigator. The first name, generally unfamiliar to the reader, seems to stand out more clearly when juxtaposed with that of Henry the Navigator, who is so well-known that to refer to him as Henrique would almost seem like introducing a new character.

CONTENTS

Preface   vii

Chapter   I.   The Vikings and Before   1

Chapter   II.   Crusaders, Reconquest, and a King   9

Chapter III.   Portugal: A Wharf between Two Seas   20

Chapter   IV.   Another Crusade and Business as Usual   28

Chapter   V.   The Reign of Dinís: Culture,
                 Commerce, and Contacts   38

Chapter   VI.   New Horizons, Alliances, and Techniques   49

Chapter VII.   Oh So Noble Commerce!   61

Chapter VIII.   An Old Road and a New   73

Chapter   IX.   Time for Conquest   83
                 Notes   91
                 Bibliography   113
                 Index   117
                 Acknowledgments   125

                 Maps
                   Portugal   14
                   Italian and Portuguese Trade Routes   23
                   Atlantic Discoveries   57

Chapter One

The Vikings and Before

Ceuta. August 21, 1415. The African sun burned deep into
Moslem and Christian, soldier and civilian, the quick, the dying,
and the dead. After one day of furious fighting, Ceuta, the
centuries-old Moslem trade center in northwest Africa, was fall-
ing to the Portuguese army of João I. Only a few of the living —
the aged, the women, and the children — and a host of Moslem
cadavers were left to witness the Christians' sack of the city.
Merchandise of world-wide origins, silver, gold, and jewelry, were
gathered in by the conquerors. Six hundred pillars of alabaster
and marble were seized by the King's second son, Pedro, shipped
to Portugal, spiritually cleansed, blessed, and incorporated into
Christian churches and palaces.

Four days later. Duarte, Pedro, and Henrique, sons of João I,
knelt in the purified and Christianized mosque to be knighted by
their father. A week later, on September 2, the Portuguese fleet
sailed home, leaving a governor and a garrison of twenty-seven
hundred to hold a tiny beachhead clinging to the rim of the
Moslem world.

Thus rudely the Portuguese announced the beginning of an
empire, as have others before and since; thus rudely their African
epic began. The path they were following was not new. Portuguese Christians had fought the Moslems for centuries. Slowly
the Moslems had given ground, and by mid-thirteenth century
they had been driven out of Portugal. The struggle continued
at sea. Now the Portuguese were carrying the fight overseas to
Moslem territory. The capture of Ceuta was a continuation of an
old policy; but it also was the beginning of a new epoch.[1]

Third among the brothers at Ceuta but first in the future
expansion of Portugal was the prince whom history knows as
Henry the Navigator. Henry saw the vision that led along the

coast of Africa; he sent out the ships to lands hitherto unknown or little known to Christian sailors. His men settled the Madeira Islands (1419-1420[?]), reached the Azores (1427-1432[?]), pushed past the "impassible" Cape Bojador in 1434, landed in the Cape Verdi Islands in 1444. Before his death in 1460, Portuguese ships had sailed as far south as Sierra Leone. By 1487 they had revealed the entire African Atlantic coastline, had rounded the Cape of Good Hope. In the next decade came Columbus's discovery of America and the start of Vasco da Gama's voyage of discovery to India — discoveries for which Prince Henry had laid the foundation.[2]

Henry's just fame has obscured an essential fact: in 1415 he was a man with a past as well as a future. Some forty years lay before him — some forty centuries lay behind. Just as the voyages of his captains would form the indispensable base for Columbus and Da Gama, so the achievements which made Henry the dominating maritime figure of his time grew from the previous experience of generations of fishermen and traders.

Why had the Portuguese gone to Africa? How had they reached it? Whence the ships? the men? the arms? the scientific knowledge that enabled them to conquer one of the strongest Moslem centers? What impelled them to attack a far more numerous people on their own soil? The answers to these questions lie in the centuries before Henry took the stage in 1415.

II

Geographically, Portugal stands at the southwest tip of Europe. This fact has suggested that it is on the rim of civilization. The Portuguese themselves speak of Cape St. Vincent as the "end of the world." But in a global concept there is no "end," only a center. If we visualize a world map projected from Portugal, it is evident why this country often has served as a crossroads where cultures mingle, change their original individual characteristics, and become something new. Since prehistory, Portugal has been in active contact with northern Europe by way of the Atlantic and with the Levant through the Pillars of Hercules.[3]

Flights of poetic fancy which made Gibraltar a formidable barrier had no basis in fact. Phoenicians, sailing into the Atlantic and leaving the Rock on their right, sought the shores of Portugal, France, and England. Portuguese artifacts dating from the Bronze Age remain to show its trade with faraway regions.[4] In later times there came the Greeks and the Carthaginians; and after them the Romans, nurturing many traditions of early trade and migrations in which legend and history are pleasantly mingled. Men moved easily in both fact and fiction in those times, and, not surprisingly, we find that a belief that Peninsulars came from Scotland and Cornwall has its converse in Irish literature, which ascribes an Iberian migration to Ireland.[5]

Roman conquest intensified contact with other lands. Language, culture, and commerce became Roman. Imperial armies were drawn from all areas. Roman inscriptions name many of those who served far from home, returning to die where their funerary monuments yield us a record we use to write these lines.

Economically, Portugal was of a piece with the Roman structure. The typical products of the peninsula — wine, oil, salt, salt meat, salt fish, smoked fish, sweet oranges, horses, wool, textiles, woods, sparto grass, wax, slaves, gold, silver, copper, tin, iron, and mercury — went to other parts of the empire by land and by sea. The merchants and shippers of the Atlantic coastline dominated the seas from Britain to Africa, possibly as far south as the Guinea coast.

When the Barbarians came to hack away the decaying timbers of empire, unity gave way before diversity in the peninsula.[6] Vandals, Alans, Suevi, and Visigoths all invaded the area early in the fifth century. They fought among themselves as much as against the Roman inhabitants. The Visigoths drove the Vandals into Africa and then gathered most of the peninsula under their rule. Near the end of the sixth century they established their capital in Toledo. They were never a united people, however, and Spain and Portugal suffered much from the civil wars over the throne.

Contacts with northern Europe such as the peninsula had known during the Roman period were greatly diminished but not lost. When Dagobert I opened a fair at Le Landit outside Paris in 629 A.D., merchants of Portugal were possibly among those named there as Spaniards, along with others from Provence, Lombardy, and elsewhere.[7]

Visigothic disunion was an invitation to new invaders, and they came — from Africa. The Moslem movement had spread rapidly throughout the Near East and across North Africa. By the end of the seventh century the Moslems had conquered Morocco, converted its inhabitants to Islam, and now looked across the Strait to Spain. A few probing movements showed the weakness of the Visigoths, who were hacking one another to pieces as usual over the kingship; and in 711 Tarik, the Moslem leader, assisted by a large number of deserters from the army of the Visigothic king, Roderic, defeated Roderic in battle. Within half a dozen years they had conquered most of the peninsula, always assisted by considerable numbers of the natives, and their victorious march was not halted until they met the Franks under Charles Martel near Tours in France in 732. Troubles among themselves in the Moslem world, rather than this defeat, forced them to retreat from France into Spain, where they established their capital at Córdova under Abd-er-Rahman I (755–788).

Most of Spain and Portugal were under Moslem rule. But not quite all. The rugged mountains of the northwest had harbored the remainder of the Visigothic nobility. They fought against, but also traded with, the Moslems. From this nucleus of Christians a new kingdom, Asturias, emerged. This kingdom, somewhat expanded, became the kingdom of León early in the tenth century. Along the east border of León was a line of castles, Castile, which emerged as a separate kingdom in 1035. Meanwhile, other Christian kingdoms, Navarre, Aragon, and the county of Catalonia, had come into existence at dates lost to history, but during the late ninth and early tenth centuries. Often fighting against one another, often associating with and marrying with the Moslems, they showed few signs of forming a union based on Christian nationalism for three centuries after the Moslem conquest of the peninsula. During the eleventh century, however, the situation gradually changed. Spain and Portugal, before the rest of Europe, were caught up in a fervor of anti-Moslem feeling. The crusading spirit spelled the eventual doom of the Moslems who still held most of the peninsula.

III

The Moslem conquest in 711 brought back to the Peninsula a trade and foreign contacts it did not enjoy during the Visigothic period. The Moslem religion and law and the Arabic language bound together a trade empire extending from Portugal through the Mediterranean, the Near East, Persia, India, China, and the Spice Islands. The Moslems brought to the Iberian Peninsula a flourishing civilization which embraced industry, commerce, and agriculture as well as the fine arts and learning. Economic and intellectual life were reoriented and intensified. Cities in Portugal and Spain became world-renowned centers of learning. But it was toward Alexandria and the Near East rather than toward west Europe that the Peninsulars now looked for their commerce. The Moslems, tolerant of their Christian subjects even to permitting them their churches, bishops, monasteries, and convents, carried on an active trade with Christian Portuguese and Spaniards. Olive oil, textiles, arms, ceramics, crystal, and paper were among the products going to Italy, North Africa, Egypt, Greece, Syria, and other places.

The south coast of the Peninsula was frequented by Moslem, Christian, and Jewish merchants. That both Christians and Moslems found commerce and religious enmity compatible is demonstrated in the reign of Charlemagne. The scourge of infidels, he scorned not to cook his food in Moslem oil, clothe his subjects in Moslem hides, and supply his scanty industry with lead and other products from Moslem lands. In many, if not most, cases, Christians and Moslems lived side by side in towns where, since Roman times, large numbers of Jews also had dwelt, all three faiths leading a common life except on Sundays, Saturdays, and Fridays when they went separate ways to worship the one Jehovah.[8]

The formation and development of Portugal can scarcely be understood without a proper appreciation of the roles of the Moslems and the Mozarabs — the Christians who lived under

Moslem rule. Although remaining Christian, culturally the Mozarabs were largely Moslem. Speaking both Arabic and Romance, they were more advanced than their fellow Christians driving on them from the north. Long before Europe re-established its contacts with the Near East through pilgrimages and crusades, the inhabitants of the Iberian Peninsula formed part of the Moslem trade world, and benefited from direct and continuous travel and trade in other parts of that vast civilization. Portuguese ports were a part of the Moslem trade empire just as Portuguese learning was a part of Moslem geographical and nautical science.

In the mid-twelfth century, the principal ports referred to by the Moslem geographer Edrisi were Silves, Alcácer, Lisbon, and Santarém; inland Évora and Elvas also were important. Edrisi dwells on the commercial activity and the shipbuilding in these centers. Of towns then in Christian hands, he mentions only Coimbra, although we know that Oporto, Viana, and other towns to the north were savouring the first profits from what was to become an active foreign commerce. Certainly it is clear that Moslem Portugal had developed trade along the Atlantic coast. Speaking of Silves on the south coast, Edrisi says, "Its figs are exported to all the countries of the Occident."

Along this Atlantic coast the retreating Moslems and the advancing Vikings met, fought, and learned from each other. For example, from a small Moslem fishing vessel, the *carib,* developed the caravel so important in later exploration. And the better to fight the Vikings, the Moslems adopted and adapted the Viking boats.[9]

IV

The maritime contacts of Portugal with Europe were never completely interrupted by Roman decline, German invasion, and Moslem conquest.[10] The Viking voyages, initiated in the mid-ninth century, were continuous and greatly influential. Many modern writers have stressed the part played by these intrepid sailors in the revival of European commerce.[11] Beginning as raiders and pirates, the Vikings gradually modified the nature of their activities until they crossed the invisible line that separates the more respectable forms of piracy from the less respectable forms of commerce. They restored the economic ties between northern and Mediterranean Europe while at the same time foraging from the Near East to New England.

The Sagas and other literature, however questionable their accuracy, preserve a memory of Portugal. It appears as "Portingal" as well as under other names. The Tagus is "Tög," Lisbon is "Lissibon," and Alcácer is "Alkassa."[12] In the *Chronique Rimée* it is recorded that Charlemagne allotted Galicia to the Flemings and Portugal to the Normans. The equally inaccurate *Gesta Caroli Magni* assigns Portugal to the Flemings and Danes.

Our knowledge of the Vikings in Portugal, though far from exact, is definite.[13] According to the Moslem historian, Ibn al Koutia, it was about 843 that they struck the Hispanic shores. They won for themselves the name of "Madjous" (pagans); and most references to the "Madjous" ended with the imprecation "May God curse them!"[14]

Viking ventures were encouraged by the growing fame of Santiago de Compostela where religious belief — formidable and frequently invincible opponent of documented history — held that the body of Saint James the Elder had been discovered in 840. Distance and rough seas did not prevent the pilgrims and the merchants from paying their respects, but they added to their prayers, "From the savage north people, deliver us." For the Vikings, the land they knew as Jakobsland was fat pickings.

The expedition of 843, or one slightly later, sacked Moslem Lisbon and continued into the Mediterranean. Another expedition about 858 struck Galicia and Portugal and continued on to Greece. It was during this same period that Viking leaders were settling down in England and France, becoming dukes of Normandy in 911.

Such raids and settlements were closely allied to the incipient commercial revival. The Vikings — raiders, pirates, and merchants — became Christians. This did not seriously hamper their style of fighting; they continued to go to Santiago. Others from the north also exchanged their products for those of the Iberian Peninsula.

Dates can be monotonous, but so must have seemed the incessant Viking raids: 961, 971, 1014, 1016 — this last led by

Olaf Haraldsson. He first struck England, killing the Archbishop of Canterbury, despite which deed he was later beatified as Saint Olaf. Raids on churches were a Viking specialty, perhaps because the churches had the most readily exportable wealth. (Or it may be merely that we hear more of such raids because the churchmen kept the chronicles.) One Viking leader, Ulf the Galician, won his nickname for his raids between 1048 and 1066. The latter date, not unknown in English history, saw the famous William of unwed parents gather his adventurers from all Europe to conquer England.[15]

In the Mediterranean, other Normans — the incredible sons of Tancred of Hauteville — were setting up a new dynasty. Reaching Apulia in Italy in 1017, they worked their way along as Christian pilgrims by piracy and pillage, living off the country, robbing the inhabitants whether Moslems or fellow Christians. The brothers liked it in Italy; they stayed on. Eventually they founded a duchy under brother Robert Guiscard, who became Duke of Apulia. In 1053 they captured Pope Leo IX; six years later Pope Nicholas II recognized Robert's title in exchange for feudal vassalage. Under brother Roger they next addressed themselves to the conquest of Sicily, which kept them occupied from 1060 to 1091. The conquest was completed at a felicitous time: Roger's Moslem subjects, fighting under Bohemund, were valiant soldiers during the First Crusade (1096–1100) to wrest the Holy Sepulchre from their fellow Moslems.[16]

As the eleventh century drew to an end, the Normans held both ends of a North Sea–Mediterranean sailing route whose feasibility had long since been proved. Portugal now stood not on the outer rim of Europe but at a midpoint which achieved greater importance with the beginning of the crusades.

In Portugal and Spain the crusades had already begun. The Norman expeditions which stopped over in Portugal represented only a part of the land-hungry thousands who burst out of Normandy, Flanders, Burgundy, and England. Into the Iberian Peninsula they poured, their greed sanctified by Christian zeal to drive back the Moslems.

Among the crusading knights was a grandson of Duke Robert I of Burgundy, a young man named Henry.

Chapter Two

Crusaders, Reconquest, and a King

Like many another young man of his time, Henry of Burgundy left home because in his native land he had become "war surplus." In the northern countries of Europe, particularly in France, England, Germany, and the Low Countries, the development of feudalism had placed strong kings, dukes, and counts in ownership of the land. Since the rules of primogeniture applied in the inheritance of the fief, younger sons were left without sufficient land to support their high titles and soaring ambitions. When they dreamed of seeking their fortunes abroad, their fathers and elder brothers were only too ready to speed them on their way.

The lands of Spain, held in large part by the Moslems, were legitimate prey, and although fertile more in fancy than in fact, they were attractive to well-trained fighting men with nowhere else to go. At the end of the century such men would flock to the Holy Land, but meanwhile the crusading spirit was directed toward Spain, which offered land here and now and a heavenly home hereafter. "Give me men and vassals," Robert of Frison, second son of the Count of Flanders, is reported to have said to his father, "and I shall go to conquer a domain from the Saracens of Spain."[1]

Two kings of Castile and León, Fernando I and Alfonso VI, were natural leaders for the young blades. Their imaginations stirred by the successes of these kings, they were ready to unsheathe their sharp points in the service of the Prince of Peace to drive out the infidel. Some of the noblest blood of the north was represented among them. Thibaud de Semur met death at Tolosa in 1065. Eble, Count of Rouci and Reims, also led an expedition to Spain about 1073 after devastating the property of the church at Reims. Able and energetic, he was well connected: his brother-in-law was Sancho Ramírez of Aragon and his father-in-law that same Robert Guiscard who was establishing Norman control in southern Italy.

Operating under the rules prepared by Hugh, Abbot of Cluny, Eble entered Spain with a veritable army, but he was not highly successful. His expedition had papal approval, bringing into the Peninsula, and eventually to Portugal, papal control over the reconquered territories. Eble was required to recognize Roman authority and pay the "dues of Saint Peter," for Pope Gregory VII claimed Spain as specifically his patrimony and forbade anyone to enter for conquest without papal consent. It was better that Spain remain under Moslem dominion, so the Pope held, than continue its Mozarabic rites after reconquest.

After the expeditions of Thibaud and Eble, there was that of Hugh, Duke of Burgundy, in 1078. Later he retired, self-blinded, to Cluny, his uncle's monastery, to make himself worthy of eternal life. In 1079, another Hugh — of Chalon — brought an expedition of crusaders to Spain and died there. He left a widow, Constance of Burgundy, who suffered no lengthy mourning and soon married Alfonso VI. Two other members of the family came to Alfonso's court: Eudes, Duke of Burgundy, and his cousin, Raymond of Burgundy. Another Burgundian, the Henry so important to our story, was a cousin of Raymond and, like him, a nephew of Constance and of Hugh, Abbot of Cluny, Abbot of Abbots.

The monastery of Cluny, founded in 910 by William, Duke of Aquitania, profoundly affected European life by virtue of being the principal single influence that elevated the papacy to its position of power from the eleventh century onward. The number of Cluniac monasteries had multiplied throughout Europe until now, in the eleventh century, the Cluny influence was felt in Spain where Fernando I and Alfonso VI helped to found, and endowed, some twenty-five such monasteries. In many cases, the monks—who were often of the same noble French families as the crusaders—aided in the Reconquest and shared in the spoils.

Of the thousands of fortune-seekers, the two most successful were the Burgundians, Raymond and Henry. As well as being nephews-in-law of Alfonso VI, both also became his sons-in-law. Raymond, who may have come to Spain as early as 1080, married Alfonso's legitimate daughter, Urraca. Henry, arriving sometime later, married Teresa, an illegitimate daughter. Raymond was made ruler of Galicia, which embraced northwest Spain and a portion of what is now Portugal. Henry became ruler of *Terra Portucalense* about 1095. This was the nucleus of the Portugal that came to be.[2]

II

Henry made Guimarães in the north of Portugal his capital. From this fortified city lying between the Douro and Minho rivers, he maintained his semi-independence from his father-in-law while carrying on his wars against the Moslems. Surviving both Raymond (who had hoped to succeed Alfonso VI as king) and the king himself, Henry supported his sister-in-law Urraca in the complicated war of succession that followed Alfonso's death. Perhaps he hoped that his territories would be extended in return for his support. At any rate, the disputed succession helped Henry and Teresa to keep in mind their task of insuring that it was they, not some other Christians, who governed the *Terra Portaculense* when the Moslems eventually and inevitably were driven out.

Sometime between 1112 and 1114 Henry died, perhaps in battle, leaving a son, Afonso Henriques, not more than four years old. Becoming regent, Teresa fought to maintain the child's claim to *Portucalense*, although there was nothing in the Spanish customs of the time to guarantee him that inheritance. Afonso Henriques was a worthy son of an astute mother and a brave father. He displaced his mother as regent in 1128, exiled her, and took over the rule until his death in 1185. Before that day came, he had established beyond a doubt that Portugal was separate, distinct, and different from Spain; and he had made himself king.[3]

During the life-span of Henry and his son, contacts were increasing between a growing Portugal and a reviving Europe.

Northern Europe's economic rebirth had been foreshadowed in 898 by the establishment of the fair at Bruges. The continued development of this region, the beginning of the fairs in Champagne from 1118 and St. Denis from 1119, and in 1121 the formation of the *marchands de l'eau* by King Louis VI (the Fat) to control the commerce of the Seine, all attested that the new age was coming.[4]

Portugal, as has been seen, was not outside this new development. Far from being inaccessible, Portuguese coasts were the haunts of northern mariners. French coins circulated in Portugal in the tenth century; French commerce came to Santiago de Compostela in Galicia and on to Portugal.[5] In 1096, on its way to the First Crusade, the fleet of Count Robert (later to be known as "of Jerusalem") followed the coast of Portugal and Spain into the Mediterranean, where it joined with that of other crusaders. The Vikings, long since Christianized, participated in the crusading movement, and in 1108 King Sigurd of Norway reached Portugal, en route to the Holy Land. He attacked Sintra and Lisbon, crossed the Tagus and attacked Alcácer do Sal on the Sado River, then sailed on into the Mediterranean. In 1111, crusaders on their way from England joined in the fight between Alfonso of Aragon and his wife Urraca of León (Raymond's widow). Acting "as if they were Moabites," profaning the churches, killing noncombatants, and raping the women, these "Anglo-Norman Pirates" were captured by Bishop Gelmirez of Santiago, who subsequently released them to continue their crusade.[6]

Thus, by the end of the eleventh century, sailing between Portugal and her neighbors was entirely feasible. A regular trade by way of Portugal later would become as important as the overland route from Italy to Flanders and Portugal's share would increase in the future, but there is clear evidence of economic development and overseas contacts from the beginning of the twelfth century. Demonstrating this is the growth of a fair and market system in Portugal, parallel with that in other parts of Europe.[7] A fair was chartered at Ponte de Lima in 1125; others were established during the century. The privileges granted the merchants in these fairs show their increasing stature. Although the geography of Portugal made her port cities more important than inland fairs, the latter too offered a variety of merchandise from the Levant and other foreign parts.

III

Portugal's position naturally impelled her toward the sea. Her people tended to concentrate around the estuaries where they could engage in both river and sea fishing. Salt for the fish was furnished by many salt pans, and eventually salt was exported. From the daily round of fishing came knowledge of the sea, weather, sailing, and boatbuilding. In this respect Portugal's development resembles that of Holland, Belgium, Scandinavia, and Italy, where the progress from fishing to coastwise trade to overseas trade was a natural sequence. If it can be said that Holland was "built on the carcasses of herrings," it is also true that Portugal owes much to the sardines and other fish off her shores.

Many ports shown on the medieval *portolanos* are not useful today, having silted up over the centuries. The Moslem geographer Edrisi says that the Minho River, which separates Spain from Portugal, was navigable as far up as Tuy and Valença, both of which had a foreign trade. Caminha at the mouth of the Minho; Viana at the mouth of the Lima; Fão and Esposende on the Cávado; Vila do Conde, Azurara, and Pinidelo on the Ave; Leça, Matozinhos, Foz, Massarelos, Oporto, and Gaia on the Douro; Mira and later Aveiro on the Vouga were all ports in the twelfth century and after. The Mondego River was navigable to small vessels as far up as Coimbra. Other ports southward along the coast were Paredes on the Liz, which with Perdeneira, São Martinho, Alfeizarão, and Selir belonged to the monastery of Alcobaça at a later date. The Italian traveler Rizo reports that Alfeizarão was an important shipbuilding center as late as the fifteenth century; in the sixteenth century its port would hold eighty decked vessels *(alto bordo)*. Atouguia and Lourinhã, both given to crusaders in 1147, were still important in the fifteenth century. Ericeira, the Tagus River and its affluents, the Coina and Sacavém, and the city of Santarém on the

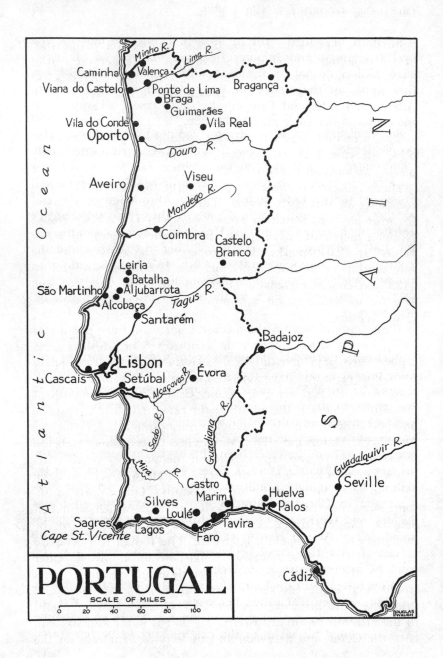

PORTUGAL

SCALE OF MILES

0   20   40   60   80   100

Tejo must be added. Still in Moslem hands for most of the twelfth century, and in some instances for half of the next, were Alcácer do Sal on the Sado, and Sines and Odemira farther south on the west coast. Lagos, Alvôr, Silves, Portimão, Albufeira, Loulé, and Faro on the south coast, all appear on the charts under their medieval names.

The principal products shipped from these ports—fish, salt, olive oil, wine, cork, sparto grass, and resins—all found a ready market in northern countries.[8]

Many indications show the presence of foreigners or foreign commerce in this early period. The price of land at Villanes, for example, was stated in French *écus*.[9] In 1130, English and Norman merchants were robbed by a Galician count of goods valued at 22,000 marks, their property being restored by the intervention of the merchants and the Bishop of Santiago. In 1138, a Genoese merchant, Guglielmo Sardena, sent his son, Oberto, to Santiago on a combination pilgrimage and merchant venture.[10]

IV

Portugal's territorial expansion continued while foreign contacts increased. Afonso Henriques was a restless, energetic, redoubtable, astute, and sagacious warrior who never ceased in his efforts to drive the Moslems back and to assert his independence from the rulers of León-Castile. His great and decisive victory of the early period was Ourique, fought in 1139, at just what spot no one has ever been able to determine for certain. In fact a small battle, it was a victory which lost nothing in the telling. Its imaginary hundreds of thousands of defeated Moslems and its Christian miracles were the very stuff of heroic history, and Ourique soon took a firm hold on the Portuguese mind. When Afonso Henriques followed up this triumph with a victory over the invading Leonese king the same year, his goal of independence seemed closer.[11]

His subjects had called him king since the death of his mother in 1130, as they had called her queen; but this title was customarily given to the daughters of kings in Spain of that time. Afonso wanted his claim to the title of king to be recognized, and may have used it as early as April 1139. In 1143 when a peace treaty was signed with Alfonso VII, this monarch was styled Emperor and Afonso was called King. But he needed recognition from a greater power as a guarantee of his independence from Alfonso VII. Since the Papacy could give him such recognition, he now turned to Innocent II. He was in a position to ask favors of the Pope, and vice versa, for Afonso had strengthened papal power in Portugal, and by degrees the popes had issued decisions which were to establish a national Portuguese church.

Papal rights in the Iberian Peninsula were not fully recognized during the early Reconquest. If papal authority had ever clearly existed before Moslem times, long Moslem occupation had left its exact extent doubtful. Furthermore, Mozarabic rites were different from those of Rome. We have noted the energetic assertions and orders on this point coming from Gregory VII in 1073. Additional complications had resulted from the rival claims of Toledo in Castile and Braga in Portugal for the primacy among the Peninsular bishops, a point of the utmost political importance. Toledo claimed primacy over the entire Peninsula; Braga claimed independence of Toledo and primacy over a number of bishoprics of Portugal and northwest Spain, including Coimbra, Oporto, and Santiago. Santiago had so grown in stature, however, that it claimed primacy over several adjacent areas, including Braga.

Afonso worked to make Braga independent and primate, subject only to the pope, and finally succeeded. He was ably aided by a remarkable church statesman, João Peculiar, whom he appointed Bishop of Braga. While Afonso by no means ended the questions of eccleciastical boundaries between Spain and Portugal, he did make definitive the existence of a Portuguese church.

The coming of the Cistercian order to Portugal about 1139 was also the occasion for greater papal control and national growth. This order of monks distinguished itself by reclaiming barren lands, of which there was an abundance in the areas disputed in the Moslem-Christian wars. Placed under papal

supervision and endowed by Afonso Henriques, they were another link between would-be king and the Papacy.

In these acts which strengthened papal authority, Afonso
sought to have his title of king recognized by the Pope. In 1143
he took another step of importance: he gave Portugal to the
Papacy and received it back in vassalage. With the Pope so far
away, he seemingly gave up nothing, but gained much if the
Pope recognized his independence from Spain. His success was
only partial. Although the Pope accepted Portugal, in his letter
of acceptance he referred to Afonso only as *Dux*. This was a
blow which Afonso ignored; his loyalty did not waver. Even
though he was not to be accorded papal recognition of his title
as king until 1179, he had laid the groundwork for the separate
church as a part of the separate nationality of Portugal.[12]

V

While battles in Latin were being waged by João Peculiar,
Afonso had not neglected the sword. Standing as a great barrier and a great opportunity was Lisbon, the Moslem stronghold of Portugal. Previously, about 1143, Afonso had attacked
it, reinforced by crusaders who paused en route to the Holy
Land. But he was not successful, and had to await a better
opportunity.[13]

During the waiting period Afonso took another step of considerable significance: in 1146 he was married to Matilde,
daughter of Amadeo III, Count of Savoy.[14] Not the fact of his
marriage, but the identity of his bride is important. Although
Italy was a long way from Portugal, the relationship between
them was already established, and this political marriage may
be regarded as pursuing the same line of policy as Afonso's
relations with the Papacy.

But neither the political nor the amorous aspects of the marriage detained Afonso for long; and he was soon attacking the
Moslems again. Santarém was taken in March 1147; Lisbon
fell to the Christian forces the following October. The capture
of this bastion of Islam in the West was a great step forward,
and had no little to do with the continued favor of the Papacy.

Lisbon's fall was brought about with the help of several

thousand crusaders. In June 1147, some two hundred ships bound on the Second Crusade arrived off the coast of Oporto carrying a contingent of men from France, England, Flanders, Germany, and other northern areas. They agreed to help capture Lisbon in return for the right to sack it. This, as we know, was the custom of Christian crusaders when an infidel city was captured (or, for that matter, a Christian city). The siege went on amidst constant bickering; at times crusaders of different nationalities fought among themselves, at times against Afonso's forces. When, after several months, Lisbon fell, the sack was carried out with great thoroughness and brutality. The murdering, robbing, and raping spared neither Moslems nor Mozarabic Christians, whose bishop was killed.[15]

Many of the crusaders settled in Portugal and many received land. Their agreement with the King allowed them to keep their own laws and customs, and granted freedom from the *portagens* and *peagens* (taxes paid at bridges and gates) in all the ports of Portugal for themselves and their heirs. As a result, they were interested in commerce. Several towns were established—or re-established—by the new settlers under grants which somewhat resembled the feudal tenure characteristic of the northern countries.

A large number of crusaders received appointments. Gilbert of Hastings, an Englishman, was made Bishop of Lisbon by Afonso, and other Englishmen, Flemings, and Germans were named canons. There was a steady influx of foreigners, small in number perhaps, but significant. Bishop Gilbert was sent to England, where he successfully recruited more fighting imigrants. Intermarriage led to increasing foreign contacts, including further marriages between the Portuguese royal family and European princes.[16]

The commercial importance of the capture of Lisbon was evident. The coast as far south as that city was now open to Christians, and also the inland area now served by the Tagus River, which was then navigable more than a hundred miles upstream. Mediterranean-bound crusaders had a limitless harbor for reprovisioning.

We have no statistics on the trade of that time. Some have held that crusading ships carried no merchandise,[17] but the greed of the crusaders taken together with the economic privileges they demanded and got would seem to belie such a view. Foreigners continued to come, and they continued to trade as well as fight. They helped in the attacks on Alcácer do Sal in 1151 and 1157 when Afonso failed to capture the city, and perhaps also in 1158 when he succeeded.

How far afield had the Portuguese wandered by this time? We cannot say; but a single fact may be of significance. A trade fair, San Demetrio, was held each year in Thessalonica. A Greek author, writing during the first half of the twelfth century, mentions Greeks, Italians, French, Spaniards, and Portuguese among the traders. It was unusual in that early time for the Portuguese to be distinguished from the Spaniards.[18]

Chapter Three

Portugal: A Wharf between Two Seas

The Portuguese merchants at the San Demetrio fair could have come there among crusaders, or they could have accompanied Italian merchants, who had been trading widely in the Mediterranean for some time. The revival of Italian commerce already had tied it by sea to North Africa and the Near East, and soon would take it into the Atlantic and to northern Europe.

Venice on the Adriatic and Amalfi on the Tyrrhenian became the early commercial leaders in Italy, both having close relations with the Byzantine Empire. Amalfi certainly, and probably other cities of Italy and the West, carried on trade with the other Moslem cities of Italy, Sicily, and North Africa. In the western Mediterranean, Genoa led the trade revival.[1] Attacked and sacked by the Moslems in 931 and 935, nevertheless it dominated the Tyrrhenian Sea a quarter of a century later. Pisa, another growing port, cooperated with Genoa in the temporary occupation of Corsica and Sardinia, 1015-1017.

This latter year, it will be remembered, saw the beginning of Norman occupation of southern Italy, and from this time on the two currents of Christian reconquest of the Mediterranean were contemporaneous. The Genoese and Pisan fleets often cooperated with the Normans. The Pisans, who captured Bona in North Africa in 1034, joined with Genoa to aid in the conquest of Palermo, Sicily, in 1072. In 1084 they burned a Moslem fleet in the harbor of Tunis, and Pope Victor III followed up this thrust by sending a fleet of three hundred ships against El Mehdia in 1087. As a result, the Genoese and Pisans received free access not only to El Mehdia but to all Tunis.

The Christians under papal auspices, far from refusing to trade with the Moslems, were fighting to gain commercial rights in their territories. The completion of the Norman conquest of Sicily in 1091 was another step forward in this Christian recovery. About 1092, Genoese, Pisans, and Catalans attacked Tortosa in Catalonia, which was then in Moslem hands; and in succeeding years there were further alliances of the three against Moslems along the coast of Spain and in the Balearic Islands.

In this period Henry of Burgundy became Count of *Terra Portucalense,* and the First Crusade began.

The Italian victories were part of a general movement against the Moslems. They had brought about a situation which enabled Christians to travel through the Mediterranean to the Holy Land. During the course of the eleventh century there were a hundred and seventeen known pilgrimages. On one of them alone, in 1065, there were an estimated 11,000 persons, many of whom traveled by sea. Before the First Crusade, Italian cities had their centers, called factories, in Constantinople and other parts of the Byzantine Empire. The crusades would stimulate Italian commercial growth and see the establishment of many more such centers with their corresponding trade privileges.

War was resumed early in the twelfth century when the privileges gained by the Genoese and Pisans in 1087 were annulled by the Moslem ruler of Tunis. After Moslem attacks on the cities of Italy and southern France, including Marseilles, Genoa declared a protectorate over these cities, and warred on Bougia and the Moroccan coast, winning new privileges in a treaty with the Moslems about 1137.

Both war and trade continued during the following years. Cooperation with Christian Spanish monarchs in attacks on Moslem Spain and the Balearic Islands brought the Italian cities new trade rights from Alfonso VII of Castile in 1146. In 1157, the Italian cities and other Christian allies attacked Corsica, Sardinia, and the Balearic Islands; in 1158, Afonso Henriques captured Alcácer do Sai on the Sado south of Lisbon, which had fallen to him eleven years before. The Moslem gap between the Christian forces was lessening.

By 1160, the Genoese had a commanding position in North Africa. In 1161, they signed an advantageous trade treaty, twice renewed by the end of the century, with the Moroccan Moslem leaders. From 1155 to 1164, Bougia was the most important port in Africa for the Genoese. Their first trip west of Bougia came in 1160; and Ceuta, on the southern side of the Strait of Gibraltar, soon took its place on the trade routes of Italian cities.

In 1162 there occurred the first extension of the Italians into the Atlantic, so far as we now know. They sailed through Gibraltar to the city of Saleh on the west coast of Africa. The Moslems called this area El-Gharb—the West. But southern Portugal was also El-Gharb—Algarve.

II

The Italians and Christian Portuguese now had indeed come near together. Logic would indicate that if the Italians had sailed into the Atlantic by 1162, they would soon be trading with the Portuguese, but no known document proves this. It seems probable, however, that Italians, Frenchmen, Spaniards, and Portuguese all mingled in the Moslem ports of Spain, Portugal, and North Africa. Though the Portuguese are not known to have been in Africa in this period, in Portugal itself the Moslems, Christians, and Jews all traded freely together, and could have done so elsewhere. This is demonstrated in the legislation of Afonso Henriques. In 1166 he granted a charter to the recently captured city of Évora. It was designed to protect commerce, and gave rights to Moslems and Jews as well as to the Christians. In 1180 he granted to the Moslems of Lisbon, Almada, Palmella, and Alcácer do Sal the right to travel freely under his protection throughout the kingdom.

The ease of communications and life between Christians and Moslems is indicated in many ways. The current money in Spain and Portugal to the end of the twelfth century was the Arab morabitino (maravedi). Documents of 1122 show that certain merchants (known as mercadores alfaqueques) who transported ransomed prisoners were exempt from port charges on

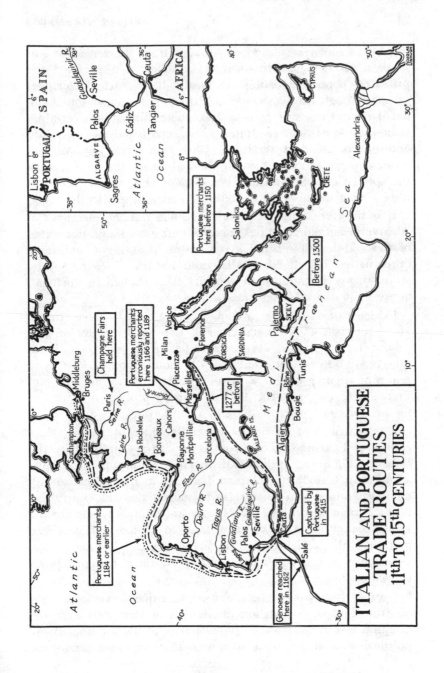

ITALIAN AND PORTUGUESE
TRADE ROUTES
11th TO 15th CENTURIES

the Mondego River for goods brought from the *terra dos sar-racenos*. Municipal ordinances of Coimbra in 1145 fixed the prices on pepper, which could hardly have reached Portugal except through Moslem trade at that date. Sugar sent to Flanders later in the century (in a Portuguese ship) almost certainly came from Moslem areas. Imports and exports moved freely into and out of Moslem territory; Christians served in Moslem armies, in government, and in the palaces of the Emirs, with the specific consent of Christian bishops and rulers.[2] Moslems were among the merchants in the fair at Montpellier in 1166.[3]

It is therefore quite possible that some Italian references to Algarve meant Portugal's Algarve. Again, no specific document of the mid-twelfth century says so. But if, as Finot and some other writers have held,[4] Italian and Flemish cities traded by sea in this period, almost of necessity they touched in Portugal, as we know the crusaders were doing.

Evidence of other foreign contacts also exists. In 1160, Afonso Henriques betrothed his daughter to Ramón Berenguer of Barcelona. Her premature death came before the marriage could take place, but the betrothal was a demonstration of Portugal's policy of aligning herself with such states as Barcelona, Aragon, France, England, and the Papacy to gain protection from her immediate and dangerous parent, León-Castile.

The marriage of Urraca, another daughter of Afonso Henriques, to Fernando II of León in 1165, was annulled by the Pope in 1175 on the grounds of the close kinship of the couple. (The long period that elapsed between marriage and annulment has caused some historians to suggest that the enmity between Fernando and his father-in-law was the real reason for the Pope's action.) In 1174, Sancho, later to be King of Portugal, married Dulce, daughter of Ramón Berenguer IV of Barcelona. Berengaria, Sancho's daughter by this marriage, became Queen of Denmark.

During these same years, Afonso Henriques never lost sight of gaining papal recognition of his title as king. Although the question was subordinate in papal policy to the solution of the political and ecclesiastical disputes that kept the Peninsula seething with hatreds and torn with wars, the political sagacity of Afonso eventually won him his wish. The jurisdictional struggle between Toledo, Santiago, and Braga had been contested with the usual in-fighting tactics and clerical backbiting understandable only to those who have followed the vicissitudes of the Papacy during the Middle Ages. Embarrassed by the claims and counterclaims of the three would-be primates, and even more by the political rivalries of León, Castile, and Portugal, the Papacy had tried to find a way through the maze. By 1179 the political situation was fairly clear: Portugal was here to stay. Although not all the dioceses now in Portugal were placed under Portuguese ecclesiastical control by that year, the political facts were acknowledged. Afonso Henriques was recognized as King of Portugal. Whether Afonso created Portugal, or whether it existed as an ethnic and national fact long before, is a question that intrigues those historians and anthropolgists who are fond of following mystical clues.

III

A marriage important politically and economically was that of Teresa, daughter of Afonso Henriques, to Philip of Alsace, Count of Flanders, in 1184. The contact which led to this marriage was made in 1177 when Philip put in at Lisbon with a fleet bound for the Holy Land. Back in Flanders, he negotiated the marriage through ambassadors sent to Portugal. When Teresa sailed to her husband's land, she was escorted by a Flemish fleet and one furnished by King Henry II of England. Henry is credited with promoting the marriage as an alliance of Flanders, Portugal, and England against Philip II, King of France, Henry's feudal overlord for the holdings in France brought to him by his marriage with Eleanor of Aquitaine. The fact that when Teresa's husband died, she married Eudes III, Duke of Burgundy, is an indication of the political importance in which the northern rulers held Portugal in this epoch.

The marriage of Philip and Teresa brought many Portuguese to Flanders. Some settled there and, with the Flemish settlers in Portugal, stimulated an already existing trade. From this Portuguese colony, established in Flanders before the end of the twelfth century, developed a *feitoria* (trading post, or factory), which still existed in the sixteenth century. This important institution will be discussed later.[5]

Meanwhile, the crusades continued to facilitate Portuguese contacts with the northern countries. The kings lost few opportunities to gain the crusaders as allies, and the Third Crusade provided another such opportunity.

Two fleets with Flemish, German, English, Frisian, French, Danish, and other crusaders put in at Lisbon in 1189. Sancho I had succeeded his father in 1185, and they joined with him in attacks which he was already preparing. The first fleet of crusaders sailed southward along the coast of Portugal, assaulting various Moslem towns. On reaching Alvôr on the south coast, they captured and sacked it, killing the inhabitants, old and young. Thereafter they sailed on to Gibraltar, where the Portuguese and some of the German ships turned back laden with the spoils of the expedition. In the same year, 1189, a second armada, consisting of English, German, and French vessels, agreed to cooperate with Sancho in the attack on Silves in return for the right to sack. The Portuguese fleet in this venture consisted of some thirty-seven *galés e naves de alto bordo* plus a number of smaller *setias,* a good illustration of Portuguese maritime growth. The siege took place amidst the usual quarrels between the crusaders and Portuguese. After the city was captured, the bulk of the crusaders sailed on, but some remained, among them Nicolau, appointed Bishop, and Guilherme, appointed Dean.[6]

A significant bit of commercial knowledge comes to us from one of the crusaders. A German who took part in the conquest of Silves reports that merchants seen in Moslem cities were subsequently seen in Montpellier and Marseilles. Did he mean merchants seen in Portugal and later in France? The Latin text is not clear. But in view of the known Italian trade with Spain and North Africa, there is no reason why southern Portuguese cities could not have been included in this trade. No known document says specifically that Christian Portuguese cities were trading directly with the Mediterranean at this time, though such trade was certainly possible.[7]

A year after the capture of Silves by the Christians, the Moslem leader Yacub Almançor brought over an army from Africa and attacked Silves and other cities, besieging King Sancho I in Santarém. Sancho was aided on this occasion by some five hundred English crusaders who were in Lisbon. The Moslems retired only to return in 1191, recapturing Silves, Alcácer do Sal, Palmela (in sight of Lisbon), and Almada on the Tagus. By this campaign the Portuguese had lost their conquests of many years back, and were to be another half century in clearing the south of the Moslems.[8]

Many of the crusaders remained in Portugal, as they had done in earlier times. And Sancho I, like his father Afonso Henriques, regarded them as desirable settlers and offered them inducements to stay. Several were appointed to high church office, as we have seen. Many were granted land secured by *forais* (charters) which often permitted the crusaders, as previously, to retain their own laws and customs. Among the settlements were Vila dos Francos (Azambuja), between Santarém and Alenquer; Sesimbra, south of Lisbon between the Tagus and Sado rivers; and others between the Tagus and Ervedal. Among the settlers there were some who had been recruited by Guilherme, Dean of Silves, in his native Flanders, and who like others before them were exempted from the *portagens* on their goods. The Cistercians were among the beneficiaries of such grants, coming to dominate a large area around Alcobaça and the adjacent seacoast.[9]

Chapter Four

Another Crusade and Business as Usual

Portugal was not to be free of the political involvement which royal marriages and foreign commerce bring to a nation. Teresa's matrimonial alliances with Flanders and Burgundy brought her native country into the contentions over the commercially important lowlands of the Rhine and the Scheldt. The kingdoms of England and France as well as the county of Flanders and the duchy of Burgundy were parties to the disputes.

The French monarchy, growing in strength, felt it necessary to control the outlets of the two rivers, and England, although only in the process of becoming a nation, already had a policy of preventing any strong power from dominating the area across the Channel. Previously Henry II had manifested a great interest in Flanders, and his son and successor, Richard the Lion-Hearted, moved to counter his fellow-crusader, overlord, and rival, Philip II of France. In 1197, King Richard bound himself by treaty with Baldwin, Count of Flanders, to join in common cause and make no separate peace with Philip.

Meanwhile, Count Philip of Flanders having died on a crusade to the Holy Land, his Portuguese wife Teresa became embroiled with Philip II of France over her rights in Flanders. In 1194, she was married to Eudes III (Odo III), Duke of Burgundy, friend of Philip II, but this did not settle the question of her property, which Philip II wanted to incorporate into his crown domains. Baldwin, the new Count of Flanders, Teresa, and Richard I (the Lion-Hearted) of England, all had need of a common front against Philip II, and this brought them into agreement.

When John became King of England in 1199 he inherited Richard's policy, but sought peace with Philip II on terms that would protect his own territories in France and bring peace in Flanders.

In the midst of his peace negotiations with Philip II, he dispatched an embassy to Portugal to ask in marriage the daughter of Sancho I.[1] He had been attracted, according to Herculano, by the descriptions of this princess. A Portuguese embassy went to England and was cordially received. But John would not have been John if he had been consistent: without waiting for an answer he married another lady who was already betrothed to one of his vassals, thereby getting himself into more trouble. The record is scanty here, so we do not know why Sancho I, a man not to be treated lightly, did not show more resentment. It seems that he had in any case refused John, which did not prevent John from addressing him that same year as "dearest brother and friend."

The significance of Portugal's involvement in northern European affairs is better understood when we remember the special importance of Flanders as a manufacturing and trade center and of Portugal as a way station en route to the Mediterranean. Flanders bought English wool; hence the interest of the English kings in cultivating the friendship of the counts of Flanders at the expense of the kings of France. By the middle of the twelfth century, the guild of Flemish merchants numbered fifty-six towns, and by the century's end, such towns as Bruges, Ghent, Lille, Douai, and Ypres, which had populations estimated at 50,000, were carrying on a European-wide trade by land and sea. In 1200, Count Baldwin issued Bruges a charter which gave it, among other special favors, the right to hold an annual trade fair, and it soon became the leading port. Portugal, as we know, was already actively connected with Flanders, by land as well as by sea.

In 1202, Philip II of France ordered all merchants going from Flanders to France, Burgundy, Provence, or "ultra montes" to go through the customs house at Bapaume. The Latin phrase may have meant over the mountains into the Iberian Peninsula, for the goods passing through Bapaume included the typical peninsular products—almonds, raisins, figs, and others frequently mentioned. Furthermore, contemporary Flemish records remark that "Limoges and Pamplona are on the main route to Spain and Santiago in Galicia." The merchants also went to such towns as Saragossa, Toledo, and Lisbon. At this same time, the Catalan merchants, who also traded with the Moslem cities in the merchandise of Spain and Africa, carried it overland to Flanders, especially to Lille. Listed as coming from Spain and Portugal in this period are sparto grass, raisins, wine, oil, figs, honey, beeswax, hides, skins, and marine salt.[2]

II

The King of Portugal actively encouraged and participated in trade. In the *foral* (charter) granted to Lisbon and Santarém in 1179, there are numerous economic provisions. For example, communications to the cities were assured by the *almocreves* (muleteers). The *cavaleiros* were encouraged to use their horses in commerce, and this led to a royal grant of the *foro* (privilege) of *cavaleiro* to the *almocreves*. The crews of the sea and river boats which supplied the cities were also granted privileged status. In royal letters patent of 1204 and 1210, we find in Lisbon an *alcaide dos navios* (commander of the ships), later to be known as *alcaide do mar* (sea), as well as an *alcaide da vila*. The markets in the cities were administered by the city government, but adjoining them, following the Moslem custom, the King had his *tendas* (stores, tents) for the *artífices* (artisans) and for sale of goods, in addition to his storehouses for the taxes collected in kind.[3]

During this first decade of the thirteenth century, John of England, understandably enough, was trying to attract the Portuguese merchants. In 1203, he granted them safe-conducts to enter, reside in, trade in, and leave England with their goods on payment of the usual taxes and customs. They were to be free of arrest for debt if they were not the chief debtors or guarantors of a debt. In a day when an act committed by one member of a national group was "redressed" by retaliation on another, such a provision was necessary to prevent their arrest for the debts of other Portuguese. John had to extend this type of protection to foreign merchants because English wool, tin, lead, and other products were exported largely by foreigners. In 1205, he granted still other privileges to merchants of Portugal and to "other merchants of Spain." In 1208, another safe-conduct was granted to a Portuguese merchant.[4] The success of the Portuguese abroad is further illustrated by the fact that a Portuguese merchant was established in Dublin before the end of the twelfth century.

Royal safe-conducts or no, piracy, frequent shipwrecks, and arbitrary arrest by local authorities put very serious obstacles in the way of trade, even down to the modern period. During the Middle Ages the situation was often beyond control. In theory, however, the king did control foreign commerce, and could thus regulate the entrance, activity, and exit of merchants. Portugal was like other nations of the time in that its merchants needed such guarantees abroad, and that its king could reward or retaliate on foreign merchants.

To protect foreign as well as Portuguese merchants from complete loss of a shipwrecked cargo, the Portuguese *Córtes* of 1211 legislated a considerable departure from custom, which hitherto had given to the king, to local authorities, or to salvagers ownership of such cargoes. The new law provided that goods shipwrecked on the coast of Portugal, whether of Portuguese or foreign ownership, should be restored to the owner and not forfeited to the crown nor to any other person.[5]

The intermingled relations of Portugal, England, and Flanders may be seen in the marriage of Fernando, son of Sancho I, to Jeanne of Constantinople, daughter of Baudouin and heir to Flanders. This marriage brought complications to Fernando that are too involved to recount here; but it also brought more Portuguese to Flanders. When Henry III of England granted freedom of commerce to the Flemish, the Portuguese merchants living there were also the beneficiaries.[6]

III

Every crusade was an intensification of foreign contacts, the Fifth Crusade, 1217, being an example. In that year a combined English, Flemish, Frisian, Dutch, French expedition (not to mention other nationalities), stopped over at Lisbon, as was by now an old crusader custom. As was an old Portuguese custom, the men were enlisted in the fight against the Moslems, the objective being that important stronghold on the Sado River, Alcácer do Sal, which had so often changed hands and which was the key to control of regions to the south. It was taken by the combined forces in October after more than two months of siege, and not long thereafter, in January 1218, the crusaders sailed on to the Holy Land. An interesting feature of this campaign was that King Alfonso II took no part in it. He busied himself in internal administration while the Bishop of Lisbon led other bishops, the Abbot of Alcobaça, the Knights Templar, the Hospitallers, and other religious orders in the attack.[7]

Portuguese trade with England seems to have been on a regular basis during this time, Henry III favoring it as he did that of Flanders. A royal order issued by him in 1220 refers to a Bartholemew of Portugal who shared equal rights with three Englishmen. In 1226, Henry issued more than one hundred safe-conducts to Portuguese merchants to trade in his territories, by which he meant his lands in France as well as in the British Isles. These permits probably were inspired by an incident of 1225 in which Englishmen had seized a Portuguese ship, the *Cardinal,* carrying a cargo of tallow and oil. The goods had been returned on the protest of the Portuguese, but the ship apparently remained a possession of the English king.

There is an interesting sidelight to this affair. While the case of the sequestered cargo was still in litigation, Henry was asked to release goods valued at forty marks for the use of six Portuguese students studying in Paris. It is not clear who they were, but we do know how other Portuguese came to be in France at that time. Powers gained by the Papacy under Afonso Henriques had come to be extremely irksome to his successors, and Sancho II (1223-1248) from the beginning of his reign had the customary altercations with the Church. One of the quarrels was over the commercial and tax privileges enjoyed by the

Bishop of Oporto. When Sancho sought to diminish these for the benefit of his own treasury, there ensued a long and bitter fight, during which the King and many of his partisans were excommunicated and many others were driven into exile. The country was placed under interdict. Sancho was forced to give in, and an accord of 1240 provided that the Portuguese merchants resident in France, those who had taken sides against the Bishop of Oporto, should be absolved.

Portuguese trade with France was not always safe from the English, not even its trade with Aquitaine and Gascony, territories subject to England. In 1242, Henry III ordered the seizure of a ship at Royan, had it conducted to Bordeaux, confiscated the cargo of rice, alum, almonds, and brazil wood, and traded a part of this cargo for Flemish cloth newly arrived. At about the same time another ship, described as Spanish, was taken. It was from Ceuta, principal western terminus of Moslem trade, whither Christian merchants resorted to buy African and eastern merchandise. Such goods were brought to northern Europe by Spanish, Genoese (?), and Bayonnais ships, which plied the Atlantic coasts with African and Levantine products.

Henry III appears to have been on a better footing with the Portuguese the next year, for he paid nine Portuguese merchants 316 livres and 7 sous for wax and rabbit skins. He borrowed 300 Bordeaux livres from a Portuguese merchant, repaying a sum described as 100 marks sterling. The merchant also received a special safe-conduct valid for six months in Bordeaux.

Some of the Portuguese ships of the period may have belonged to the King himself. We have already noted that he carried on commerce in the markets. The King's *taracenas* (shipyards) already existed in Lisbon in 1237, and may have been there longer. This is indicated by a custom, apparently dating from the beginning of Sancho II's reign, which required the Jewish community to furnish every new ship belonging to the king with anchor and cable. During the reign of Dinís (1279–1325) there was a complaint that the custom had not been enforced. A *pretor* of *marinheiros* (seamen) governed the King's shipyard

in Sancho II's time, and during the following reign of Alfonso
III (1248–1279), the *marinheiros* of Lisbon had their own
judge, the *alcaide do mar,* of earlier origin. Soon the seamen of
other cities had similar officials.[8]

IV

The reign of Afonso III saw notable progress in commerce
and foreign contacts. Before becoming king, Afonso had lived
for many years in French exile. The nephew of Blanche of
Castile (wife of Louis IX [Saint Louis] of France), he was
married to Mathilde, Countess of Clermont en Beauvoisis, and
was made Count of Boulogne. Afonso had been greatly im-
pressed with French court life, and brought back from exile a
taste for Provençal poetry and other features of French culture.
When he married Beatrice, daughter of Alfonso X (the Wise)
of Castile, he came under another important foreign influence.
Both of these cultural currents would have a profound effect
on the life of the heir to the throne, his son Dinís. Afonso
imported tutors from France, among them Aimeric d'Ébrard of
Aquitaine, for Dinís who showed a great capacity to benefit from
his education.[9]

Numerous Portuguese merchants now lived abroad in Flanders, France, England, and elsewhere. In Sevilla, shortly after
its capture by the Christians from the Moslems in 1248, there
was already a street called Calle de los Portugueses. They also
had their own chapel, San Francisco, described as magnificent.

The king as business man again appears on the scene. Afonso
III bought or constructed houses, stores, workshops, and inns
for rent. Such economic ventures — perhaps the term capitalistic
might be applied to them — were regarded as normal for the
Portuguese royalty and nobility, even when land remained the
principal source of income. The lack of any prohibition on
commerce for them was no small factor in the subsequent
expansion of the country.

An Afonsine law of December 1253 reveals the economic
status of Portugal at that time. Attempting to stop a trend of
rising prices — which a modern economist might call an inflation
caused by flourishing business — Afonso III fixed prices on some

four hundred items, many of foreign origin. Among those listed were iron, copper, brass, tin, lead (raw and manufactured), arms, fine woodwork, linen, silk, and a variety of other cloth, including English and Flemish scarlet (*escarlata*) and the dyed cloth of Rouen and Ghent. The main countries of origin of the imports were England, France, and Flanders. Castile and Andalucia were mentioned, as they and adjacent Spanish territories frequently were in economic matters. Among the cities specified were London, Ghent, Rouen, Ypres, Commines, Abbeville, Lille, Saint Omer, Chartres, Tournois, Montpellier, Valenciennes, Segovia, and Toledo.

The justification of the law of 1253, leaving aside any theoretical discussion of its efficacy and wisdom, was the rise in prices, which went higher than in former epochs. The amount of money in circulation was greater, and many taxes hitherto paid in kind were now paid in specie. Money was inflated also by the royal right to "break the currency" every seven years — that is, the king could debase the coins. Afonso met with such opposition in 1253 that he desisted; but when 1261 came around he issued new, debased coins.

V

A necessary part of national growth in this period was the reconcentration in royal hands of the personal and collective privileges held by the nobility, the Church, and even merchants. Numerous internal customs lines existed, duties being collected quite legally by bishops, religious orders, priors, abbots, nobility, and cities; many others collected duties by usurpation. As the nation developed, conflicts ensued, especially with the churchmen.[10]

A case in point is the struggle between the Bishop of Oporto and Afonso III. Oporto had been the patrimony of the bishops since granted to them by Teresa in 1120. As the port grew in importance, they collected revenues on commerce which the King regarded as his own. The establishment across the river of a royal village, Vila Nova de Gaia, had not been a success, and while the city of the bishops prospered, that of the King languished. Afonso's efforts to divert some trade and customs from Oporto were resisted by the Bishop, who rose in arms. Defeated, he appealed to the Pope, who upheld him; but Afonso III won by standing on a new law enacted on March 17, 1254. It provided that goods coming from up the Douro should discharge two-thirds in Oporto and one-third in Gaia; while all vessels large and small from France and other ports outside the river Douro should discharge half and half, in Oporto and Gaia. Vessels belonging to Oporto were allowed to discharge there.[11]

Either in this same year or the next, the King forbade the export of silver in bars, money, or objects. Furs, colored cloth, leather, wax, and honey could be exported only through ports which received cloth of France.[12] Another law attributed to Afonso's reign speaks of Portuguese "além mar ou em França," an expression believed to refer to Africa as well as the northern countries (but this is hardly conclusive proof that Portuguese went to Africa to reside so early).[13] In 1258, wax, skins, and leather went to England, and numerous Portuguese received permission to come there to trade.

Flemish trade is shown in a document of May 1269 listing the tax known as *petit tonlieux* on products of Castile, León, Andalucia, Granada (Moslem), Galicia, and Portugal. The products imported are about the same from all, including honey, wax, skins, leather, ointment, oil, figs, raisins, sparto or Spanish grass, and a variety of coloring matter. The Flemish exports to Portugal included farm and manufactured products, among them horses, oak wood, cloth, dyed cloth, and dyes. The English trade both ways was similar, though it is only later that the existing documents consistently show all these products.

VI

Several types of Portuguese ships were used in this epoch. Among those mentioned are the *caravel, barca, barco, nave, baixel, pinácia,* and *barcos saveiros.* Although it is difficult to know precisely what is meant by all these names, they are listed as engaging in fishing, navigation, and commerce.

Afonso III showed his interest in commerce by improving some of the harbors, Vila do Conde being an example. In 1260, he gave a house evaluated at 160 Portuguese pounds to João de

Mina for his service in constructing a ship, presumably for the royal fleet. Certain records of this time listing the tithes and port dues paid the king on foreign cloth, metals, foods, arms, wood, and other products apparently date back to Sancho II.

Further legislation concerning the *alcaide do mar,* the seamen's judge, is connected with the appearance of an official known as the *corretor,* whose function was to act as a broker to speed commerce. The ship broker, *corretor de navios,* facilitated loading and discharging ships, while the customhouse broker, *corretor da alfándega,* aided clearance of the goods.

Another indication that direct trade with the Moslem lands existed is found in the *foral* of the port of Viana, 1258–1262. The residents of the region were excused from paying the *portagem,* while the *dízima* was collected only on goods from France and the lands of the Saracens. This is one of the few direct statements showing such trade. No part of Portugal remained in the hands of the Moslems at this date, and no adjacent part of Spain was in their possession. We must conclude that Viana, a port in northern Portugal, carried on a sea trade with the Moslem lands.

Moslem trade was considered merely a continuation of what had been customary when they occupied a portion of Portugal. After the Christian conquest of the infidel territories in 1249–1250, the products of the area continued to be exported to their usual Moslem markets and were paid for in goods and in Tunisian *valedias,* which circulated in Portugal.

This widespread Portuguese trade was soon to lead to the development of new trade institutions.

Chapter Five

The Reign of Dinís: Culture, Commerce, and Contacts

The reign of Dinís (1279–1325) was a notable epoch in the development of Portugal.[1] His father, Afonso III, had implanted the germ of French culture. One of his teachers, Aimeric d'Ébrard, was subsequently Bishop of Coimbra and a founder of the University of Lisbon (later moved to Coimbra). Before its establishment in 1290, young men of Portugal went to study at Montpellier, Paris, Bologna, Salamanca, or elsewhere. The foreign influence on Portugal had been strong, perhaps most notably in law: Roman law as revived by the medieval scholars had furnished a basis for royal power. Furthermore, a considerable number of Portuguese bishoprics had been filled by foreigners. But with the founding of the University of Lisbon, more young men were trained to become a part of the corps of *letrados* and *legistas* (men of letters and law) so necessary to the running of a government.

Roman law also had come to Portugal through Spain. Relationships between Portugal and Spain were close, even in the midst of numerous wars. During Dinís's reign the noted commentary on Roman law by Jacome Ruiz, *Flores de las leyes,* was translated into Portuguese. Perhaps on the initiative of Dinís, who was the grandson of Alfonso the Wise of Castile, Alfonso's *Siete partidas* was also translated into Portuguese; it circulated in Portugal by the year 1341. Dinís, in fact, made Portuguese rather than Latin the language of law, thus creating, however unintentionally, an additional instrument of patriotism, nationalism, and royal growth. He also helped in the creation of a national literature. Himself a poet, Dinís cultivated writing poetry in the Provençal style, which had been among his father's imports from France, and a school of Portuguese poetry grew up around him.

The Order of Christ was another of his profoundly vital institutions. From the earliest periods, the military orders had their counterparts in Portugal, among them the Spanish orders Santiago and Calatrava, and the Hospitallers and Knights Templar throughout Europe. When Philip IV of France secured the dissolution of the Knights Templar early in the fourteenth century, Dinís was able to persuade Pope John XXII to give their holdings to an order specifically designed to protect the Christians from the raiding Moslems. The Order of Christ was endowed with ample property, including the stronghold Castro Marim near the mouth of the Guadiana River on the Spanish border. By the time Henry the Navigator became Grand Master a century later, the order had developed a tradition of being Portugal's chief anti-Moslem offensive weapon; and Henry was able to use its resources in the wider field to which his greater imagination carried him and his country.

Commerce and agriculture also received the aid of the industrious Dinís. King of a sea-minded people, he was one of the most apt of a line of commerce-minded monarchs. Sizing up accurately the favorable geographic position of Portugal for trade, he set himself to improve on nature's gifts. The pine forests of Leiria are an example of his farsightedness. There were (and are) great dunes of sand lying along the coast north-ward of Lisbon, stretching up and beyond Leiria. Here Dinís planted pine forests which, while growing into timber for ship-building, served as windbreaks, providing protection for the inland farms.

Farms, ships, and trade: all benefited at his hands. Privileges were extended to the trade fairs which had been in existence for a century; new charters were granted to newly created fairs, among them "free-fairs" with special status. Foreign trade was encouraged and commercial development stimulated in ways which will be described in more detail hereafter.

Dinís made his reign notable for its wide foreign contacts with Italian cities, France, England, and Flanders; and he knew

how to absorb from them the elements which prospered his own
nation. Utilizing all the resources at his disposal, he created
trade institutions which would still be of importance centuries
later.

II

Before the time of Dinís, the Portuguese, as we have seen,
were trading with northern Europe. Portuguese, Spaniards, and
Moslems are listed among those having trade with Bruges in
1252. In 1280, special privileges were granted to those called
"Spaniards"; and it is clear that this name included the Portuguese.[2] A tribute to their well-known diplomatic abilities, recognized even at this early date, may be seen in the settlement of a
dispute which arose between the foreign merchants and Robert,
the Seigneur de Ghistelles, in 1281. The Lord of Ghistelles held
in fief the grounds on which the public weighing was done at
Bruges. His use, or abuse, of this privilege brought him into
conflict with the foreign merchants, who appealed to the overlord, Count Gui de Dampierre. The merchants of the Hanse as
well as those of the Iberian Peninsula appointed the Portuguese
as their representative to the Count. Together with the City
Council of Bruges and the Lord of Ghistelles (who perhaps was
forced to join in), Count Gui issued an ordinance satisfactory
to the foreign merchants on May 26, 1282. He also persuaded
Robert of Ghistelles to sell the grounds to the city in February
1293, making the area a *franc-alleu*.[3]

Simultaneously with the development of its Flemish trade,
Portuguese commerce was expanding internally and in foreign
areas other than Flanders. In 1282, Dinís extended the same
privileges already granted to the mariners of Lisbon to the
mariners of Tavira and Lagos, cities on the south coast, long-
time centers of Moslem trade before Algarve fell to the Christians. Lagos and its noted seamen were to become the backbone
of Henry the Navigator's activity a half century later. We may
note here — and it may appropriately be repeated later — that
Dinís's action in 1282 demonstrates the Christian continuation
of the Moslem African-Mediterranean outlook which characterized Algarve when it was still in Moslem hands.[4]

Portuguese overseas trade was, nevertheless, predominantly northward-looking and would remain so for many years to come. Portugal still traded mostly in the products of her own soil. At a later period this fact was less true and less important, but if we are to understand what was happening in Portugal at this time it is essential to know why so much depended on her domestic products. A contrast may help to show the reason.

Nearly all the international trade of Europe had been carried on in the temporary fairs, of which Champagne became the most famous. The goods exchanged were mainly foreign, brought from regions far apart to a convenient meeting ground. Since almost any place easily reached would have done as well, few permanent cities of size and wealth resulted from such fairs unless other favorable conditions were present. The Italian cities also became largely merchants of goods brought from abroad to be exported again. But only the few really good ports located at the head of convenient land routes became the permanent cities.

Portugal combined the advantages of good ports, incoming foreign goods to be exported, and, most important of all, domestic products in demand in northern Europe. Her commerce did not suffer the fate of the shifting and temporary fairs. Portugal's trade and cities grew; the importance of the trading element grew. Moreover, the people who produced the goods, the owners of the land, the very same nobles who surrounded and helped the king, themselves became merchants of their own products. Merchants and nobles, though in most cases members of different classes, had an identical interest — to sell their produce abroad. Furthermore — and it is a point of so much importance that it must be frequently repeated and placed in its context — the King of Portugal was king of both the merchants and nobles, not of the nobles alone. How could he avoid being merchant-minded? Is it strange that he should become a merchant himself? And so, the best markets for the products of Portugal being overseas, the initial advance was in that direction. This can be shown in still another way. Behind Portugal, inland, Spain produced the same commodities — wax,

cork, oil, wine, honey, dried fruits, salt. But whereas Spain had
a long land boundary connecting her with her best markets,
France and other northern regions, Portugal was compelled by
her position to look overseas for her markets. Lisbon, Porto,
Setúbal, Lagos, Faro had more contacts by sea than by land.

III

Consequently, it is overseas contacts which provide the key to
Portugal's growth as merchandiser and monarchy.[5] In 1283, for
example, the Corporation of London appointed brokers to
handle the incoming merchandise from Portugal; five years later
such brokers were again named. What the Portuguese were
bringing into England at this time was not specified.

Santarém, just above Lisbon on the Tagus, was trading overseas with France, Algarve, Sevilla, possibly Africa. The French
side of this trade is revealed by a letter patent issued to the
Portuguese merchants resident in Harfleur. In January 1290,
Philip IV guaranteed their personal safety along with privileges
designed to protect their property. Such guarantees had to be
frequently repeated because they could not be easily fulfilled.
The wars between the rulers, as well as the never-ending chain
of reprisals carried out by one nationality or city against the
citizens of another, made the merchant's lot difficult. With
declared wars, undeclared wars, and outright piracy, merchants
who sailed the seas risked their lives and property with every
toss of waves that were indeed stormy.

Portuguese merchants, both as aggrieved and aggressors, were
involved in the disputes that were inseparable from commerce
and international relations. Even the greatest determination on
the part of kings and merchants to keep the peace would
probably have failed, and there is no indication that they were
more peaceable than others. In any case, trade and politics both
brought entanglements. Their trade with England was carried
partly in their own ships and partly in Gascon and Spanish
ships. The Gascons and Spaniards were bitter rivals whose
frequent disputes embroiled their sovereigns in England and
Castile. Portuguese ships plied the waters of Spain, Aquitaine,
France, Flanders, and England. England supplied wool to

Flanders. English subjects (Aquitanian merchants) were among the most aggressive in the coastal trade to northern Africa, where they were rivals of the Spaniards as well as of the Portuguese. While still cultivating the friendship of England and Flanders, Dinís nevertheless maintained vigorous protection of his men.

Portuguese-Gascon rivalry grew toward the end of the thirteenth century, straining the best intentions of Dinís to maintain friendly relations with England as expressed in his numerous letters to both Edward I and the future Edward II. He complained that contrary to the promises of the English King his merchants were often molested in Aquitaine or England. Edward in his turn complained that pirates sallied forth from Portuguese ports to attack the English (Aquitanian) ships en route northward with their cargoes from Africa. Furthermore, foreign merchants in Portugal sometimes had to take sanctuary in the churches to save their lives. As the accusations of both monarchs were true, the customary retaliations by both sides, whether by royal order or on individual initiative, kept the quarrels and fights going. Thus — to take only the area of Europe that for the moment interests us most — an informal but destructive commercial and maritime war was being carried on between the Aquitanians and the Spaniards on one side, the Aquitanians and the Portuguese on another, and the Portuguese and the Spaniards on a third. Always, of course, to the accompaniment of assurances of peace, good will, and future fair dealings!

IV

One of the complications of the problem was that Portuguese goods and merchants often traveled on Spanish ships, and vice versa. Dinís placed the blame on the Castilians in 1293; Edward rejected the explanation, but promised to force his subjects to keep the peace and asked Dinís to do the same. In a move toward peace two Aquitanians and two Portuguese were appointed to settle the disputes. If they could not decide cases arising between the Portuguese and Edward I's subjects, the respective kings were to appoint others. A one-year truce was declared, with safety promised for merchants of both parties, the Portuguese promising not to travel or trade in Castilian ships. As an interested friend of both parties, the Count of Flanders was called on to arbitrate in February 1294, and peace was arranged after negotiations that lasted into 1295.

But peace was a relative term, then as now. On October 3, 1295, Edward I approved a letter of marque which had been issued by the Duke of Aquitaine to Bernard Dongresselli, a merchant of Bayonne. Forced into Lagos by storm while en route from Africa, his ship had been taken to Lisbon where the cargo was tithed by the King and the remainder seized by Lisbon merchants. The letter empowered him to seize Portuguese goods to the value of 700 *libras*. And so it went.

In the midst of such events the Kings of Portugal and England exchanged congratulations on the long-standing friendly relations that existed between their merchants. And their relations *were* friendly — in a relative sense.

V

The difficulties and dangers of trade by sea could be overcome only by the combined action of the King and his merchants, and so we may attribute to such difficulties the most important advance then made in the economic institutions of Portugal — the creation of the *bolsa de comércio* on May 10, 1293.

Sometime before this date, the merchants had made a compact (*pustura*) among themselves. They agreed that all vessels of 100 tons or more loading in Portugal for Flanders, England, Normandy, Brittany, and La Rochelle should pay a tax of twenty *soldos* sterling, while those of less tonnage should pay ten *soldos*. Also, the same tax should be paid by vessels chartered by Portuguese merchants to go *além mar* (overseas), to Sevilla, or elsewhere, and which went to Flanders or any of the above-mentioned regions. From the sums so collected, 100 marks silver or the equivalent was to be kept in Flanders and the balance in Portugal, to be spent in legal defense or in other ways needed for the common cause of the members of the compact.[6] Any owner refusing to pay was subject to a fine of ten pounds sterling.

The King approved this compact, which added an extra measure of enforcement. To us it shows a degree of commercial organization not known elsewhere in Europe except in Italy, and it illustrates the mutual interests of the King and his merchants, perhaps unique at the time. The compact establishing the *bolsa* in Flanders was a step in the formation of the Flemish *feitoria,* the factory house or trading post where Portugal worked out many of her trade techniques and laws for dealing in overseas affairs. No area of Europe outside of Italy had more experience than Portugal in this field, and Italy failed to develop the unified kingdom needed to back up her merchants in the even more intense rivalry of the fifteenth and sixteenth centuries.

VI

The need for such measures of protection and all others that could be found is shown in the history of the period that followed. Those were the years which saw the Kings of France and England, Philip IV and Edward I, locked in warfare, with Castile generally on the French side and Portugal favoring England. Sometimes the Kings hired or requisitioned ships from other nations for their fight, as in 1295 when Philip requisitioned the foreign ships in his ports. Seven from northern Spain were among them. Whether any were Portuguese is not certain, but in 1295–1296 two Portuguese ships were in Philip's navy.[7]

The war brought about, or at least aggravated, the friction among the merchants. Dinís, calling attention to the harm thus done, appealed to England and France to make peace. But it was another case of the doctor not liking his own medicine. In 1295, Dinís intervened in the family strife in Spain, made a short truce, then renewed the war, which continued into 1297. As one result, there was trouble between the merchants of the two countries. A bloody fight broke out in Lisbon in 1296 between the local merchants and those of northern Spanish cities. Each side suffered a number of dead and wounded, and each seized the goods of the other.

After peace was restored between the merchants on January 22, 1297, there was a mutual restitution of goods, payment for the dead, and care of the wounded. The truce was signed by the

Câmara (City Council) of Lisbon and by the representatives of the *Hermandad de las villas de la marina de Castilla* (Confraternity of Castilian Seaports), which was organized in 1296 to protect the interests of the maritime cities against their own king and others. The Spanish merchants "now in the port of Lisbon" agreed to leave eighteen hostages as a guarantee that Portuguese goods would be returned to Lisbon, La Rochelle, Normandy, or Flanders. Apparently both sides were satisfied to renew "the great love which for long had prevailed" among them, for in 1297 we find some twenty-six Spanish ships anchored at one time in the port of Lisbon from which they carried goods to their own cities, to Normandy, Flanders, and elsewhere. Did the monarchs have a hand in this treaty? Possibly; but peace was not restored between them until September, when King Fernando IV of Castile agreed to marry a Portuguese princess and his sister to marry a Portuguese prince. Fernando, the oldest of the four, was not quite twelve years old.[8]

Edward I of England had continued to encourage both the Portuguese and the Spaniards in the midst of their war. At the request of the Count of Flanders, in February 1297 he issued safe-conducts for merchants of both countries, requesting equal treatment for his own. A dispute between Edward and his own merchants because of their opposition to the foreigners led to his annulling their charters. When he restored the charters in 1298, the London Corporation at once renewed its restrictions. In 1300 they laid a restriction on the Portuguese merchants requiring them to lodge in private houses instead of their own hostels; this enabled the English both to supervise the Portuguese and to profit from housing and feeding them. The Portuguese, however, benefited from Edward's *carta mercatoria* issued in 1303, which allowed them and other foreign merchants to reside and trade in England, and to enjoy the protection of its laws. It was a salient feature of the act that in legal cases involving foreigners half the jurors were to be foreigners.

In 1304 we find a confirmation of the products which went from Portugal to the northern areas, in this case specifically to Flanders. A law of that year specifies the minimum wholesale lots of various goods which might be sold in the market of Bruges. Listed from Portugal in addition to the usual peninsular products is *malagueta* (grains of paradise), a highly prized spice of western African origin. This date precedes any known direct Portuguese settlements in Africa, and it may be presumed that the spice came via Moslem traders.[9]

VII

Two other important acts in the following years show the increasing stature of Portugal in foreign trade. The correspondence between Edward I and Dinís had been maintained, and when Edward II acceded to the English throne in 1307, he inherited the correspondence also. One item concerned a pirated cargo brought into Lisbon and claimed by the Castilian king, but which Dinís had held for two years awaiting claims from the English who might have owned some of the pirated goods. In 1308, Dinís called attention to the "long friendship" between their merchants and granted new safe-conducts for English subjects in Portugal. At the same time he asked that the English not take reprisals on the Portuguese for certain acts committed by Castilians who, he said, flew the Portuguese flag while attacking English ships. Edward II's answer was conciliatory. What is more, the exchange of letters in fact constituted a treaty, the first between the two nations: although Dinís and Edward were only confirming an understanding already reached by the merchants among themselves, their mutual promises of indissoluble friendship were the stuff of which treaties are made.[10]

France could not afford to be behindhand in this trade rivalry. The long embroilment of Philip IV with Flanders, with England, and with the Papacy had done serious damage to the fairs of Champagne and foreign trade. The question of taxation had led to the contest with the Papacy which resulted in its capture by France in 1307. The war with England had shut off most of the French coast from easy access to the sea. The Flemish question and the consequent wars in the north of France forced the merchants who had customarily gone to Champagne to seek an alternative place of trade.

Early in 1310, Philip IV compensated in part for this loss by

granting to the Portuguese, long established in Harfleur, Rouen,
La Rochelle, Abbeville, and Boulogne, further privileges and
guarantees. In addition to the usual rights to enter, reside, trade,
and leave with their goods and money, they were exempted from
seizure of goods even in time of war, and from the customs and
taxes usually paid by foreigners. They were also granted the
right to appoint and dismiss their own shipbrokers. Their
importance may be judged by another privilege they enjoyed
about this time — in Rouen they had their own cemetery.[11]

Portugal's interest in French and Flemish trade was now
intensified. But the fortunes of its merchants and of the merchants of the Spanish cities were still subject to the hazards of
the Franco-Flemish wars. Consequently, in 1317 the sovereigns
of Portugal and Castile joined together in an effort to mediate
between the King of France and the Count of Flanders.[12]

The year 1317 was notable in Portugal for another reason —
Manuel Peçanha, Genoese, member of a family of rich merchants, was appointed Admiral of Portugal.

Chapter Six

New Horizons, Alliances, and Techniques

Events were to prove that the guiding star of Portugal was in the south, and the coming of Manuel Peçanha betokens the future orientation of her policy. Henceforth, although without as yet perceptibly shifting from the profitable northern routes, Portuguese commerce and Portuguese political interests took new directions. Ever flexible in their eagerness to learn from others, the Portuguese absorbed much from the Italians, whose commercial expansion had brought them to the shores of Portugal before the end of the thirteenth century.

When the Genoese breached the Strait of Gibraltar in 1162 and started their trade with the Atlantic coast of northwest Africa, they were but a day's sailing from Portugal's southern coast, still in Moslem hands. Direct trade with Portugal was now possible, but probably did not begin until later. The Genoese traded freely with the Moslem cities, fought with them, and made commercial treaties with them. Moslems on both sides of Gibraltar were in constant communication.

The primary problem of the Italian cities still was to establish their supremacy over the Moslems, and they pursued with vigor their twofold task of driving the Moslems back and trading with them. A treaty Genoa made with the Moslem ruler of the Balearic Islands in 1181 was renewed seven years later. By its terms Genoese vessels were free from attack during their voyages to and from Spain, El-Gharb, and elsewhere, and were not required to pay a toll (*diritto*). The products which Genoa bought were carried to Italy, and to Egypt, Syria, and the Black Sea for exchange against the merchandise of those regions.

From a treaty between the Genoese and the ruler of Morocco

we can confirm that they were already established in Ceuta in 1191. Their trade with this city, Tunis, Spain, and El-Gharb included the export of such items as amber, coral, and a variety of glass work, in exchange for sugar, wax, woad (a vegetable dye stuff), skins, elephant tusks, cloth of goat hair, and gold dust.[1] Genoa's course to Ceuta via intermediate ports along the coast of France, Spain, and Africa became a source of wealth and development.

II

The thirteenth century was a time of accelerated Italian development, with Italian sea power and commerce dominating the Mediterranean. The centers of trade shifted from the Levant to Italy, southern France, and Spain, largely because of the influence of that western invasion of the East which we customarily call the Crusades. Also, Christian reconquest in Spain and Portugal left the Moslems with only Granada on the Iberian Peninsula after the middle of the century.

The increase in commerce was accompanied by better trade techniques. Written contracts between merchant and shipowner replaced oral agreements, and incidentally produced the notarial records from which the modern economic historian obtains much of his material. The companies of rich merchants drew up specific contracts with the shipowners, and these were duly notarized in Genoa, Venice, Montpellier, Marseilles, and dozens of other cities.

How early did the Italians push north along the Atlantic coast of Spain and Portugal? No certain answer can be given. A Genoese vessel was in La Rochelle in 1232, according to the Italian historian Canale, but this could hardly represent a regular trade. Both southern Spain and Portugal were still in Moslem hands up to 1248, and given the active trade of the Italians with Ceuta and of the Portuguese with northern centers during this period, there was little incentive for Italian merchants to venture farther north. Both the Moslem and Christian merchants, who welcomed Italian trade as far as Ceuta and Gibraltar, would have seen direct trade as a menace to their own activities.

A new situation was produced by the Christians' capture of
Sevilla in 1248 and the expulsion of the Moslems from Portugal's Algarve the next year. Except for Granada, the entire
European coastline was in Christian hands. New opportunities
opened up which the Italians were quick to exploit. In Sevilla
a Genoese colony sprang up, to be followed soon by a Genoese
consulado on the *Calle de Génova*. Other foreigners were there
also, including Germans, English, Catalans, French, Lombards,
and Portuguese.

Thus, it may be noted, trade carried the Italians regularly
through the Strait of Gibraltar into the Atlantic. The vessels of
the Zaccaria brothers, for example, sailed a route to Mallorca,
Almería, Málaga, Sevilla, Cádiz, and Ceuta. We also know of a
merchant of Genoa who made a voyage in 1253 as far as Safi on
the African coast in the latitude of Madeira.

The Venetians also turned their commercial eye westward
after 1261. Having lost control of Constantinople that year, they
became more interested in the trade which they had hitherto
been too busy to pursue. The fact that their enemies had been
aided by their archrival, Genoa, gave added impetus to their
urge to extend to the western Mediterranean. Genoa was push-
ing harder than ever for her trade, and to improve her relations
with the Moslems had established a chancellory with Moslem
teachers.[2]

April 17, 1277 is the sailing date from Italy of the first known
ship to voyage from Italy to Flanders. An Italian ship was
allegedly in La Rochelle as early as 1232, but we have no
definite information on the years between that date and 1277.
In 1278, five Genoese merchants chartered two ships from
Beneditto Zaccaria and one from Niccolo Zaccaria *per andare
ad partes angliae* (to go to Anglian regions). This same year a
Genoese, one Dom Vivaldo, "citizen of Lisbon," was taking part
in that city's affairs. To have achieved citizenship he must have
lived there for some time. Furthermore, it would be strange if
he were the only Italian to have established himself in Portugal
by this date, considering that Italian commerce with Ceuta was
more than a hundred years old and that Italian settlement in
Sevilla and Cádiz dated back a quarter of a century.

Some historians have speculated on the reasons for what they regard as the "late" arrival of the Italians in the Atlantic trade. If Portugal was trading actively with the north, as she was, from the twelfth century; and if the Italians were trading with western Africa, as they were, why not Italian–North Sea trade earlier? The answer to this, for those who must regard 1277 as late, is that Europe was still only in the early stages of its economic recovery from the medieval doldrums. The markets in the north could not yet absorb enough to make the long trip pay.

Several fleets in succession followed those of 1277 and 1278. We learn of Genoese vessels in the north in 1281, 1287, 1304, and 1306. These were armed vessels, carrying both sails and oars. The galleys of Beneditto Zaccaria were still active at the end of the century, for in 1298 they coasted Spain and Portugal en route to Normandy and Flanders. Italians were resident in Bordeaux at the turn of the century.

Mallorca sent ships to England in 1281 and 1304. Catalans were resident in England at least as early as 1303; a Catalan ship sailed there in 1311.

From 1293 on the archives of Venice register an annual *galere di Fiandra*. Small wonder that the Venetians were now interested in the northern sea route. At about this time there were already permanent "factories" of numerous different foreign merchants in Bruges, among those listed being Germans, Spaniards, Biscayans, Aragonese, Catalans, Italians, Sicilians, and Portuguese. In a different category were the moneylenders of Lombardy, Florence, and Siena.

The northern trade definitely paid, and what had once been confined largely to the peoples along the Atlantic was now the objective of all. Philip IV of France employed Italian shipbuilders in 1293, and hired a Genoese fleet in 1295. This is precisely the period in which he also employed Portuguese ships in his wars.[3] Genoa and Venice, already locked in desperate commercial war at the end of the thirteenth century, carried their hostilities into the North Sea. There, in 1306, their merchants fought a naval engagement.

Among the Genoese who sailed to England during this year were Manuele and Leonardo Pessagno. Not in the least backward in their economic methods, the Italians went into the interior of England where they bought up wool from the manors and monasteries. They also became bankers to Edward I and some of his successors, taking a mortgage on the customs until the debts were paid. To assure themselves of their money, they became the customs collectors. These procedures often angered the natives; in 1311 they led to the expulsion of some Italian merchants amid the rejoicing of the people, and to a serious attack on Venetian galleys in 1319. The Venetians refused to come to England for many years thereafter, sending their cargoes to Flanders to be loaded on Flemish or English ships for transshipment. But many Italians fared better. Antonio Pessagno was designated by Edward II as "king's merchant" and referred to as *carissimus mercator noster*.

The Italian fleets and Italian merchants had reached a point at which their history was to intertwine closely with that of Portuguese shipping and trade, and to influence greatly the development of Portugal. As the fleets left Italy, they touched at the Balearics, North Africa, Spain, and Portugal en route to France, England, and Flanders. Lisbon and Cádiz are often named as stopping and provisioning stations, though other towns also appear in the records.[4]

The Venetians were among the foreign merchants already established in Portugal. In 1308, during a war with Venice over possession of Ferrara, the Pope issued a bull requiring Christian rulers to seize the Venetians and their goods. King Dinís of Portugal responded in 1309 by ordering a census of the Venetians. Since no document has been found to indicate the sequel, some historians concluded that perhaps Dinís actually expelled them. The absence of any mention of Venetians in important concessions made to Genoese and others strengthened this view, but recent publications show them in Portugal after 1309; and two documents found in the Venetian State Archive, dated 1374 and 1375, refer to the "long-standing friendship" of the two peoples. The Venetian fleets, furthermore, watered and provisioned in Portuguese ports as they passed.[5]

Portugal was now so vitally concerned in this Mediterranean–North Sea trade that she could not ignore events seemingly far away. Every war between England and France, or France and Flanders, affected Portuguese trade, as in 1315 when King Louis X (the Quarrelsome) of France forbade the Flemings to come to the Champagne markets. Portugal was immediately adversely affected. We have seen Dinís and the King of Castile joining to mediate between Louis and the Count of Flanders in 1317.

But Portugal was to profit also. Cutting the land route stimulated the water route. Portugal was in the middle. Dinís invited Manuele Pessagno (Peçanha, in Portuguese) to Portugal.

IV

Manuel Peçanha[6] belonged to a prominent family of Genoese merchants, long familiar with Portugal and the Atlantic route to the north. His brother was Edward II's *carissimus mercator noster.*

On February 1, 1317 Dinís and Peçanha signed a contract which was destined to be a landmark in Portuguese history. Peçanha was to bring twenty Genoese captains to command the King's ships, and he was to maintain them at his own expense except when in the King's service. For this he would receive 3,000 *libras* a year, plus certain specified properties and the right to carry on commerce with Genoa and other places. In additional contracts signed later, there were further privileges granted, among them the appointment of Peçanha as *almirante-mor* of Portugal in perpetuity for himself and heirs.[7]

Whatever the reasons that impelled Dinís to bring Peçanha to Portugal, one thing should be borne in mind: the Portuguese were not landlubbers who were to be taught to sail. They had long since built and sailed ships that could withstand the angry Atlantic; and none knew the route northward better than they. As the Genoese and Venetian galleys rowed along the coast from Portugal, they were following a path well known to the Portuguese since the twelfth century.

Dinís may well have had much to learn from his new *almirante-mor*. All Europe recognized Italian seamen as the masters of their trade, and all Europe copied their mercantile methods. Dinís, who was a man of flexible and open mind, did likewise. He was willing to learn, and enlisting the Genoese was only one more example of his policy of assimilating the knowledge of other European countries to promote the advancement of Portugal. The Portuguese could and did learn from the Italians; but they were advanced students, not novices. To speak of them as "receiving their maritime education from the Italians," as some writers have done, is an exaggeration. Both the Portuguese and Italians made such contributions to the maritime history of the world that neither need seek to detract from the other.[8]

Many Italians were in Portugal at this time. One Eannes Cotta became Governor of Santarém, his family later being ennobled. Some of Peçanha's captains who won distinction left families in Portugal. The Peçanha family itself henceforth played a major role in Portuguese economic and political life, their descendants remaining there to our own time.

The task of Manuel Peçanha was to build up the King's fleet. To accomplish it he brought ships from Italy. He was also to improve shipbuilding, an art already well developed and one to which Dinís had given attention and support from the first days of his reign. Since money was needed for the task, the King sent Manuel Peçanha and Gonçalo Pereira to the Pope at Avignon to solicit funds for building the fleet. It was to be used against the Moslems, so we can connect it with the establishment of the Order of Christ, another act which Dinís also secured from the Papacy. Being directed against the Moslems, both enterprises had a crusading aspect. But they had their economic side as well, for whatever the theories about saving Moslem souls, there was no hesitancy about trading for Moslem goods.[9] Trade and war went together; and there was a regular business in ransoming of Christians from Moslems and Moslems from Christians.

Merchandise secured from the Moslems as well as Portuguese goods found outlets in the north. By an act of March 1324, for example, the *concelho* of the city of Oporto entered into an accord with the *homens-bons* of the city to regulate the French trade, Normandy being named as the particular destination and origin of their ships. And the next year, when Afonso IV had succeeded to the throne of Portugal, Edward II of England directed a letter to him on behalf of his sergeant-at-arms who was en route to Portugal to buy wheat and other edibles. English records of the period list many merchants with Portuguese names trading in England. The Portuguese are also named among the nations enjoying most favored trade privileges in France. An example of the commerce-mindedness of the monarchs is an agreement of 1327 involving France, England, Castile, Aragon, Sicily, and Mallorca: it concerns permitting their respective subjects to trade freely with one another by land and sea.[10]

The pattern of mutual concession to foreign merchants by European monarchs was well established, the Portuguese, as we have seen, both giving and receiving such privileges. Large numbers of individual passports were granted by Portugal to English, Flemish, French, and other merchants: but if general privileges had been granted by this date, no record of them has as yet been found. The first such concession is a milestone in Portugal's economic history.

V

The first to receive this sort of general charter were the Bardi family, famous Florentine bankers whose activities covered the Mediterranean world. They obtained a charter of privileges in 1338. Through their representative, one "Berengel onberte," as named in the Portuguese parchment, they had petitioned for "liberties" (exemptions), and were granted the right to live, trade, travel, and discharge cargo in all ports, have their own consul, and be exempt from the king's corsairs unless carrying prohibited goods to the Moslems. This charter was not unlike that already granted to the Portuguese by both the English and French. It became a model for subsequent grants to foreign merchants, the English, French, Piacenzans, Cahorsins, Milanese, and others citing it when petitioning the Portuguese crown for trade rights.[11]

Portuguese friendship was now more important than ever to

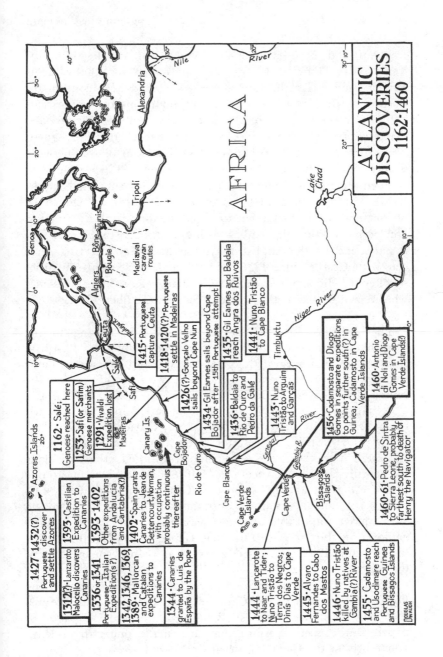

ATLANTIC DISCOVERIES 1162-1460

AFRICA

Nile
River
Alexandria
Genoa
Bône · Tunis
Bougie
Algiers
Tripoli
Ceuta
Salé
Safi
Madeiras
Canary Is.
Cape Bojador
Rio de Ouro
Cape Blanco
Cape Verde Islands
Cape Verde
Bissagos Islands
Senegal River
Gambia R.
Niger River
Lake Chad
Timbuktu
Azores Islands
Mediæval caravan routes

1427-1432(?) Portuguese discover and settle Azores

1312(?) Lanzaroto Malocello discovers Canaries

1336 or 1341 Portuguese-Italian Expedition(s?)

1342, 1346, 1369, 1389 · Mallorcan and Catalan expeditions to Canaries

1393-1402 Castilian Expedition to Canaries

1393-1402 Other expeditions from Andalucia and Cantabria(?)

1402 Spain grants Canaries to Jean de Bettencourt, Norman, with occupation probably continuous thereafter

1344 Canaries granted to Luis de España by the Pope

1162 · Salé; Genoese reached here

1253 Safi (or Safim) Genoese merchants

1291 Vivaldi Expedition, lost

1415 Portuguese capture Ceuta

1418-1420(?) Portuguese settle in Madeiras

1426(?) Gonçalo Velho sails beyond Cape Nun

1434 Gil Eannes sails beyond Cape Bojador after 15th Portuguese attempt

1435 Gil Eannes and Baldaia reach Angra dos Ruivos

1436 Baldaia to Rio de Ouro and Pedro da Galé

1441 Nuno Tristão to Cape Blanco

1443 Nuno Tristão to Arguim and Garças

1444 Lançarote to Naar and Tider; Nuno Tristão to Terra dos Negros; Dinis Dias to Cape Verde

1445 Alvaro Fernandes to Cabo dos Mastos

1446 Nuno Tristão killed by natives at Gambia(?) River

1455 Cadamosto and Usodimare reach Portuguese Guinea and Bissagos Islands

1456 Cadamosto and Diogo Gomes in separate expeditions to points further south(?) in Guinea; Cadamosto in Cape Verde Islands

1460 Antonio di Noli and Diogo Gomes in Cape Verde Islands(?)

1460-61 Pedro de Sintra to Sierra Leone, probably farthest south to death of Henry the Navigator

DOUGLAS
MCLAUGHLIN

England and France, who were embroiled in the Hundred
Years' War. Edward III of England recognized the value of
having friends like the Portuguese who could help contain the
Castilians while at the same time supplying useful imports.

Philip VI of France, in 1340 and again in 1341, affirmed and
extended the privileges previously granted to the Portuguese,
promising not to molest them even in the event of war between
France and Portugal. By these concessions Philip sought to
compensate his own merchants for the losses sustained in the
battle of Sluys, June 1340; to gain the support of Afonso IV
of Portugal, who was known to his contemporaries as a warrior;
and perhaps — though vainly — to induce the Portuguese to take
a stand against the English.[12] Afonso had been carrying on a
war with Castile since 1336, and he made peace only in order
to offer a solid front with the Castilians against the Moslems,
who were defeated at the battle of Salado, October 1340.

VI

The African coast of the Atlantic was beckoning to the
seamen of that epoch. Many new products from the East and
from Africa had suggested to the Italians and other merchants
that greater profits awaited the men who could get to the
source of the coveted spices, cloths, precious woods, and gold.

Perhaps as early as 1270 the Genoese sailed into the Atlantic
beyond Safi where their trade customarily carried them. In 1291,
the Vivaldi brothers set out for India along the African coast.
Although it was lost, the expedition stimulated others to make
the venture. In 1312, Lancelloto Malocello gave his name to one
of the Canaries, and held the island for a number of years. A
scarcity of documents and contradictions in the few that do
exist render impossible an exact account of this early Atlantic
exploration, but it is certain that Genoese, Mallorcans, Anda-
lucians, and Portuguese had a try at it before the middle of
the century.

No effort will be made here to settle a controversy about the
Portuguese voyages to the Canaries (and Madeira and Azores?)
that has consumed (almost literally) thousands of pages of
paper. But it seems certain that they made one trip at least,
apparently to the Canaries, in either 1336 or 1341.

The Portuguese claims to the islands were expounded to Pope Clement VI by Afonso IV in 1345 to counteract a grant of the Canaries made by the Pope to Luis of Castile in 1344. Whatever conclusions are drawn from the hazy and highly conflicting claims by various parties in that period, one boast made by Afonso IV seems justified. No other mariners of Europe, he said, were superior to his own. But none of the expeditions — Portuguese, Italian, or other — led to effective and useful occupation of the Atlantic islands or the African coast by the Europeans. What was needed for this achievement was an economically profitable outlet and source, and a political organization to back the merchants. The Italian city-state was never equal to the task, England and France were as yet too far away, and Castile too busy with internal problems. Portugal was not yet ready. The unveiling of the Atlantic was to wait.

But the elements for future Atlantic exploration were being assembled. Dinís had formed the Order of Christ, specifically designated to combat the Moslems. Later he received papal permission to collect special taxes to build an anti-Moslem fleet. In 1341, this fleet had joined with the Castilians, Aragonese, and Genoese in the war against the Moslems. And now, in 1345, Clement VI granted to Afonso IV the tithe of extensive church properties in Portugal to enable him to continue the war against the Moslem Benimerines with whom the other Peninsular monarchs had a ten-year truce.[13]

VII

Meanwhile, Portugal's seafaring was to be done mainly along the well-known and profitable northern trade routes. The trade was active, as the extensive records of friction between the merchants of the various nations show. Seizure of goods, reprisals, and appeals to the respective kings for protection were all the order of the day. Politics and commerce were the closest of bedfellows. When ordering the release of a Portuguese ship which the thorny Welsh had taken, Edward III stated that he did so "because the inhabitants of the land of Portugal are in the king's friendship and in the enmity of Philip of Valois, his enemy." The mere cataloguing of such events would take a prohibitive amount of space. Each incident was soon followed by apologies or excuses.

During the 1340's the monarchs of England and Portugal were in frequent correspondence; and in 1347 an attempt to arrange a marriage between an English prince and a Portuguese princess failed without causing ill feelings. Such diplomatic exchanges enhanced the value of Portugal to France, if her friendship could be secured. In 1350, Jean II of France took the usual method of confirming and extending former privileges. Still another extension came in 1353.

The English-Portuguese treaty of 1353 was to prove the more important. The merchants of Lisbon and Oporto, disappointed at the failure to bring off the marriage of the Prince of Wales to Leonore of Portugal, sought on their own to strengthen their position. One of their objectives was to have a secure and friendly England on their port side as they sailed their cargoes to Flanders. Obtaining from Afonso IV letters in which he assured Edward III that he had taken all English merchants under his special protection, they went to England and secured from Edward similar promises for the Portuguese in the English realms. Furthermore, they informed Edward that special envoys were coming to conclude a treaty. Although the envoys arrived with credentials signed only by the merchants, not by Afonso IV, they concluded a treaty to guarantee safety to the merchants of both countries for a period of fifty years. The signers on the Portuguese side were merchants, mariners, and *communidades da marinha* of Portugal, but Afonso IV recognized their signature as binding on the nation.[14]

Portugal was developing the qualities which were to be needed for the coming great epoch. Without the sort of merchants who could sign treaties on their own, there would have been no age of exploration; and without a line of kings strong enough to aid and organize them, there could have been no such body of merchants. This is not to say that Portuguese success in exploration is due to the merchants alone. It is not. But it does point to an essential element in this success: Portugal advanced more rapidly than any other nation in Europe toward the mobilization of *all* the factors needed to support a strong national action of the type required to build an empire.[15]

Chapter Seven

Oh So Noble Commerce!

Back of the port cities of Portugal, back of Lisbon, Oporto, Setúbal, Faro, and Lagos, lay the rolling plains of the south, the valley of the Tagus, and the mountains of the north where most of the people lived and worked. Their history is engrossing, but it touches our subject in only one essential particular — they produced the cork, oil, wax, wine, and fruits which Portugal exported. But although they were the producers, the owners were the gentry — the nobles, the religious orders, and the king. From the coast and the sea came two other products often exported, salt and fish, and these also were owned largely by the nobility or clergy. The people knew little of the preoccupation of their rulers with the marketing of the fruits of their labor. Foreign affairs touched them when the Castilians invaded, but — visibly — at few other times.

Seldom in history has a landed nobility been so closely associated with the marketing of the produce of its holdings. Seldom have kings been so concerned with the commerce and processing of their country's crops. However often this fact is mentioned, it bears repetition. And the years of Pedro I (1357–1367) and Fernando (1367–1383) were to see in Portugal an even greater development of the wide economic contacts which underlay the nation's future expansion.

Pedro I was a man of vigor and violence, best known to history as the king who allegedly enthroned the cadaver of his murdered mistress (or wife?), Inez de Castro, slain at the behest of his father, Afonso IV. He is also remembered by the Portuguese as the king who beheaded two nobles for killing a Jew, who castrated another noble for adultery, who whipped a bishop for the same offense, and who sired a bastard, the future King João I, while acting the part of the inconsolable lover of Inez.

It is understandable why the chronicler Fernão Lopes wrote: "The people say that such another ten years there never were in Portugal like those in which the King Pedro ruled." The vigor which Pedro thus demonstrated in personal matters also characterized his economic policies. He knew where the interests of his nobles and merchants lay and sought to promote them.

During the first year of his reign he reaffirmed the privileges of the Peçanha family, still important in Portugal and still well connected in Genoa. Many Italian merchants were now settled in Portugal, having received privileges modeled on those given to the Florentines in 1338. In confirming these, Pedro named the Genoese, Milanese, and Piacenzans as well as the Cahorsins. It should be noted that trade with the Moslems was continuing. When a merchant of Oporto died in 1359, his possessions included sugar from Bougia in North Africa. He also had 600 *libras* lent out at interest. In 1361, the city of Oporto could boast that it had "more *naves e navios* than the whole kingdom." The next year Pedro confirmed the privileges previously granted by his father to the Catalans and Mallorcans, referring in his grant to their "long residence" in Portugal and the aid given to the King.[1]

Foreign merchants were frequently troublesome, even if desirable. In 1363, the Italians whose privileges had been confirmed by Pedro refused to accept a king's *carregador* (wharfinger) to supervise their cargoes and forced the King to permit them to name their own man, as had been the custom. On the same day that they did so, the English received another charter. What one got, the other demanded.

Abroad, the Portuguese followed suit. In 1362, King Jean II of France had shown his wish to favor the Portuguese by confirming the privileges of the merchants living and trading there. In 1364, Charles V of France extended previous privileges, to which he added, among other things, tax exemptions and guarantees against high rents, personal injury, bad debts, and unfair weights. The Castilians got the same guarantees.

Since the natives received no such privileges, in Portugal, as elsewhere, they were often in dispute with the foreign merchants and their own king over the abuse, or alleged abuse, of those privileges granted to the foreigners. Pedro had to re-enact previous laws prohibiting or limiting the right of foreigners to retail their own imports or to buy and resell within Portugal. He sought to protect the foreigners by permitting them to have their own supervisors for the discharge of their cargoes; and Pedro's successor, Fernando, provided for right of trial of English merchants before his own Judge of the Customs House to protect them from the ordinary courts. Later other foreigners received the same concession.[2]

II

When Pedro died in 1367, his handsome son Fernando became king. No later king of Portugal ever chose to call himself Fernando. There is a reason why. And yet Fernão Lopes could say of him: "Standing in a large group of men, although not identified as king, he would at once be recognized as the king over the others." Few men ruled with more vigor and brought more disaster to their countries, or more good.

The little we know of him is revealing. He was first in making war, and first to retreat from the scene of battle. He fought Castile three times, sometimes dismissing his own supporters while the enemy he had incited to attack him captured and sacked his own cities, among them Lisbon. He seemed a coward, and temporarily infected his soldiers with his own cowardice — the same troops who on other occasions proved themselves the master of a foe several times their number.

He was handsome. He had mistresses. He chose as his queen Leonor Teles, a Spanish lady of lower degree than nobility; she was the mother of two children, but he boasted that he had found her a virgin. Although she had issue after their marriage, contemporaries believed that Fernando might not be the father either of them or of his mistress's children. With great secrecy he had installed in one of his palaces a Spaniard, João Fernandes Andeiro, whom he used as a diplomatic agent to the English. But it was no secret that Andeiro cuckolded the King, and he was commonly supposed to be the father of Beatriz, the heir to the throne. The King ennobled Andeiro. For his diplomatic services?

But Fernando looked like a king, and a king he was in economic matters. His economic legislation makes him the equal of the other monarchs in his line, a notable one; and his nation can afford to forget his weaknesses. Even the disastrous wars he provoked were to have a happy outcome — the accession to the throne of Fernando's half-brother, João I, father of Henry the Navigator.

On becoming king, Fernando was faced with the usual task of examining the laws and concessions of his predecessors. The privileges of Admiral Lançerote Peçanha were confirmed in 1367 and 1368, in time for Fernando to get aid from Genoa for the first of his three ill-starred wars with Castile. The Portuguese lost the war, but it is impressive that they were able to assemble thirty-two *galés* and thirty *naus* for an attack on Sevilla in 1369. The war also caused damage to Genoese shipping, for which Portugal made restitution. An extensive list of the goods involved exhibits Portugal as a center of exchange of merchandise from numerous towns of northern Europe. As a part of the peace treaty, Fernando agreed to marry Leonor, daughter of Henry II of Castile. Instead, he married Leonor Teles, and made attacks on Castilian ships along his coast, thus provoking a second war.

Trade continued with Moslem territories in Africa and with Granada — a city with which Fernando had not hesitated to ally himself during his first war with Castile. Relations with England continued friendly in the spirit of the pacts of 1308 and 1353, despite the usual incidents between merchants. Among the towns named in the British trade with Portugal we find Bristol, Bornstaple, Exeter, Dartmouth, Fowey, Plymouth, Weymouth, Southhampton, Lynn, Chichester, and others, including London, where the Portuguese lived and traded.[3]

The intensive foreign trade of the nation and Fernando's wars may have left some time for further Atlantic exploration, but if so, Portugal's primary interest continued to be commercial rather than venturesome.[4] Portugal was approaching the political and economic maturity which would enable her to break out of the European confines, but she had not yet reached it.

Perhaps Fernando had the ships and the men to anticipate Henry, but he chose instead to make a second war on Spain.

The second Spanish war strengthened the English compact. Fernando asked aid of England, finding an able ally in John of Gaunt, Duke of Lancaster, who claimed the throne of Spain through his wife Constance, illegitimate daughter of Pedro the Cruel. Only three years before, Fernando had made war on Spain to sustain his own claims to the Castilian throne.

England could use an ally at this moment: the Hundred Years' War was going badly and Castile was an ally of France. But Fernando was of little help. Spain invaded Portugal and captured Lisbon on February 23, 1373, Fernando apparently inspiring even Admiral Peçanha to play an unheroic part. The ensuing treaty required Portugal to resist the English when they arrived. Nevertheless, England and Portugal signed a mutual assistance treaty in June. The next year Fernando sent ships to help France against England.

But Fernando was busy about matters of more lasting importance to Portugal than his wars. It might be said that his impulses were warlike but his heart was in commerce. The King himself was an owner of merchant ships which carried on trade under the direction of his appointed officials. He accepted no cargo from others until he had finished loading his own, but when his merchants protested he modified this rule, saying that his policy was to promote the riches of his subjects. This was true; but we should note that he was a shrewd dealer, who anticipated some modern economic policies. The *Côrtes* of Lisbon of 1371 complained that he requisitioned wheat at five *soldos* in order to sell it again for five *libras* (a ratio of one to twenty).[5]

III

Portugal was one of the busiest marts of Europe. Some four to five hundred ships loaded annually there, according to Fernão Lopes, who describes Lisbon as being a city of "numerous and various foreigners," among whom he names the Lombards, Genoese, Milanese, Catalans, Biscayans, Mallorcans, Aragonese, and "others." The others would have included Venetians, Florentines, Piacenzans, Flemings, French, English, and Cahorsins. The value to Portugal of these "numerous and various" foreign contacts can hardly be overstressed. They brought knowledge of happenings and developments throughout Europe, and of any new trade products or lands reported.

Fernando often was called on to revise the old regulations concerning commerce or to issue new ones. In 1372 he regulated freight rates to France and Flanders at the request of the merchants, who complained that high charges levied by the ship-owners were pricing them out of the market. In the same year he heard another complaint from the *Côrtes* of Oporto that the citizens of that city and Gaia were cutting ship timber from lands belonging to others.

The profits to be made from trade attracted all classes. The *Côrtes* of Lisbon of 1371 asked royal protection from the clergy and nobility who were taking advantage of their respective priv-ileges to avoid the taxes paid by the merchants. The next year, meeting at Leiria, the *Côrtes* made complaints against the King, the Queen, the grand masters of the various religious orders, the bishops, the clergy in general, the knights, and such government officials as accountants, scriveners, customs collectors, and magis-trates (*corregedores*), for becoming "merchants and hucksters" in the port cities.

This action of the *Côrtes* calls attention to a development of significance in Portuguese society — the growth of the class known as *letrados* (the literate). Among them were the *legistas,* those learned in the law, who had become indispensable in the running of the state. Nor could the nobility and the merchants run their affairs without such men.

Not infrequently of the non-noble class, the *legistas* staffed the chancellory which prepared state papers, occupied judicial positions, held appointments to numerous government offices, and on many occasions served as ambassadors to foreign courts. Many who began as scriveners became royal advisers, forming an intermediate class between commoner and noble. Supplanting in part the noble in government, they gave a direction and continuity to state affairs more disinterested than that provided by nobility and clergy. However, many were sprung from the merchant class and were consequently commerce- and urban-minded. While they could not have cast many votes in a democratic system, they exerted a weight far out of proportion to their numbers in a society where the last word was with the king, even if at times he had to use an army to enforce it. We may say that they represented the spirit of civil and secular government in contrast to the noble and clerical. They were the commercial and urban in contrast to the agricultural and rural.[6]

Little by little, the Portuguese state was changing to accommodate itself to a new economic and social structure. In the port cities, dominated by the wealthy merchant class, the relationship between rich and poor differed from that between noble and peasant in rural areas. Although the nobility and the clergy engaged in commerce, the propertyless poor of the cities believed that the merchants represented their interests and that the nobility was their enemy. While such a proletariat could not vote, when the occasion demanded, it could be incited to riot.

These classes were the new Portugal, to which the clergy and nobility tried to belong by becoming merchants. All represented Portugal's future, which was overseas. But "overseas" still meant the old seas — the familiar, profitable routes.

IV

The passion for trade explains why Portugal became more nationalistic. The King saw foreign merchants as friends to whom he must make concessions in order to ask for similar privileges for his own merchants abroad. But the merchants wanted to have it both ways: they wanted the privileges they had been granted abroad denied to foreigners at home. And it was easy to make a case against the foreigners who enjoyed privileges which the Portuguese did not. Exempt from many taxes, free in many cases to price their goods at any price they could get while paying as little as possible for Portuguese products, they also had facilities for exporting their currency contrary to law.

Other monarchs before Fernando had heard such complaints, but they were now sharper. In 1375, the King tried to lessen

foreign competition for his merchants without destroying foreign
trade. In general, such laws — whose complex details can be
omitted here — limited the foreigner in retail trade. Legislation
of this kind was common at the time, similar laws being enacted
in Castile, France, and England. But the foreign merchant
continued to thrive, as subsequent complaints prove.

From 1375 until the end of Fernando's reign eight years later,
the King and *Côrtes* distinguished themselves for their economic
legislation. In the various acts which followed the original restrictions, it is demonstrated that the royal objective was to
promote commerce. The customs act of 1377 (*foral de portagem*) was an attempt to regulate matters then in dispute among
native and foreign merchants. Containing a list of articles a
hundred pages long, it fixed the duties on both foreign and
domestic products. Other laws concerned the measurements for
cloth, the purchase of sailcloth for the king's ships, smuggling,
and the export tax on salt shipped to France, Flanders, and
England.[7]

The stimulation of shipbuilding was the objective of an act of
June 6, 1377, regarded as one of the two most important economic acts of Fernando's reign. It provided a type of subsidy for
shipbuilders. All merchants, citizens, or residents of Lisbon who
would build ships of one hundred tons upward were permitted
to cut wood free of charge or tax in the royal forests. They were
exempt from the tithe on wood, iron, or sailcloth, even if
imported. The purchase or sale of such ships was free of tax, as
was that of a ship bought abroad. The owner or merchant was
free from all taxes on the first cargo shipped from Portugal, and
from half the tithe on the cargo returning to Portugal. The
builders or owners were excused from owning a horse or from
military service on land or sea, except with the king personally.
They were also exempt from a number of other taxes and
services imposed by the municipal council, and from taxes of the
same types on their property abroad. If the first ship built or
bought should be lost on the first voyage, the shipowner had
three years to build or buy another, while receiving the same
exemptions. A concession by the Pope the same year continued

the right, originally granted as an aid in building ships, to collect the tithe and retain half of it for conquests in Granada and other non-Christian lands. In December 1380, the privileges granted to builders of ships of one hundred tons upward were extended to those citizens and residents of Lisbon building fifty-ton ships or buying them from abroad. In March 1381, Oporto received the same privileges.

The second of the two significant economic acts was the formation of the *companhia das naus* sometime before December 1380. The *companhia* represented a form of compulsory maritime insurance applicable to all decked ships of fifty tons upward. Lisbon and Oporto are specifically named, but the law applied to all ports of the realm. It embraced the King's ships, numbering twelve. All ships were required to register their value, price, and date of construction. Each was to pay two per cent on the value of its cargo into the *bolsa* (treasury) each trip. By this payment, the owner was insured against losses in time of war or peace, and could collect for damages, losses, and other expenses as, for example, unexpected foreign taxes. If the treasury became low, additional assessments in the same proportion would be made on all shipowners. The law contained extensive technical details, recalling the "fine print" in a modern policy.[8]

The terms of the law indicate that it was a renewal, not an original act. Its prototype was the *bolsa* approved by Dinís in 1293, thus permitting us to presume a century of experience, whether continuous or not we do not know. Some historians have emphasized the need for experience to fix the percentage fees and other technical matters.[9] Years later, in 1397, when João I reconstituted the *bolsa* in Oporto after the interruption caused by the change from the old royal house to his regime, he emphasized that the fee should be compulsory if a majority of the shipowners agreed, as "was always the custom during former reigns."[10]

Portuguese maritime insurance law possibly had a wider European influence — at least in the opinion of one modern Belgian economic historian — because of Portugal's continuous contacts with both Mediterranean and north European ports.

"From the fourteenth century," remarks Goris, "Portuguese shipping developed the rudiments of modern maritime insurance. Under the auspices of the king of Portugal, entrepreneurs without a par in economic history, they had solved step by step all phases of this complicated problem. . . . The detailed and well-rounded regulations established by Fernando exercised a capital influence on the formation of maritime law in the Mediterranean."[11] Though this statement somewhat minimizes the priority generally conceded the Italians, we may nevertheless regard the insurance laws as showing the vitality of Portugal. May we also point out once more that the kings usually were merely legalizing what the merchants already had agreed to? The merchants, foreign and Portuguese, who devised the agreements traded in all parts of the European world. Since their knowledge was a common currency circulating among them all, it is very difficult to attribute unique ideas to any one group.

That the trade of Portugal was prospering during these years is abundantly clear. Some of this we know from the numerous complaints made by all parties — the Portuguese against the English and the French, and the English and French counter-complaints. One controversy which arose between the French and Portuguese in 1380 continued for several years. The French complaint was that the Portuguese merchants were free of tax in France while the French paid a tax in Portugal. The Portuguese appealed to ancient treaties, which provoked a French reply that the more privileges given to the Portuguese in France, the more hostile to the French they became, even to fighting for England against France. The Portuguese answered that up until this episode they had traded more continuously with France than anyone else.

Thanks to his legislation, King Fernando was accomplishing one of his chief objectives, perhaps the chief one. A chronicler writing a few years later says of the revenues: "They were so great, that it is now difficult to believe."[12]

V

Fernando could not bear up under such prosperity. For him it had been a long time between wars — six years since the

Castilians had captured Lisbon. And so, although Portugal had been helping Castile, and England had been giving the Portuguese some troublesome times, he decided to renew the war with Castile. Enrique II of Castile had just died, and the new king, Juan I, was thought less capable of defending his realm.

The plan was roughly the same as that of the previous war. The Earl of Cambridge, uncle of Richard II, would bring a thousand men-at-arms and a thousand archers to join the Portuguese in an invasion, and would claim the throne for John of Gaunt and his Spanish wife. The Earl of Cambridge's son, Edward, would marry Fernando's daughter, Beatriz, and they would inherit the Castilian throne. Richard II sent the beforementioned João Fernandes Andeiro to negotiate the treaty of alliance, which he did, and also used the occasion "for the easy task of seducing the queen," as one Portuguese historian remarks.

Juan I now claimed the throne of Portugal, and all parties squared away for a war which produced little fighting except a naval battle won by the Castilians in the summer of 1381, before the English fleet and troops arrived. In August, Beatriz and Edward were formally betrothed in a ceremony "as realistic in matrimonial symbols as the age of the infants permitted." However, John of Gaunt was to fail in his bid for the Portuguese throne. The English soldiers' conduct toward the Portuguese women was such that there was almost as much war between the two allies as with the Spaniards. Seemingly neither side wanted a battle, and in September 1382, Fernando secretly made peace with Juan I, magnanimously arranging a free ride home for the English army on Castilian ships.

Fernando next betrothed Princess Beatriz to Prince Fernando of Castile, but saw a better opportunity when Juan I became a widower, and ended by bestowing her hand on that monarch instead. Beatriz, who was now eleven, had been engaged five times.[13] Perhaps Fernando thought he was solving the problem of Portuguese-Castilian rivalry. And so, in part, he did, but not in the way he intended.

The marriage settlement of Juan and Beatriz produced little but trouble for Portugal. It provided that if Fernando left no

sons, Beatriz would become queen; and that during her minority
Fernando's Spanish wife, Leonor Teles, was to be regent. Since
that was an epoch when many princesses died early, there was
also a provision that if Beatriz predeceased her husband, Juan I
would inherit.

And so, having steered the ship of state straight for the rocks
and tied the helm fast, Fernando set sail in October 1383 on
what we shall hope was his heaven-bound galley.

Chapter Eight

An Old Road and a New

Leonor Teles assumed the regency as Fernando had willed, but his plan of succession got no further. The omnipresence of Andeiro, Leonor's alleged lover, was enough to arouse the people of Lisbon. A foreign queen with a foreign lover offended both their nationalism and their moral sense. They were ripe for revolt, awaiting only a leader. In the person of João, an illegitimate son of Pedro I, they soon found him. Or perhaps we should say he found them.

João was the Grand Master of Aviz, a strong military-clerical order. As well as having the people on his side, he was favored by the merchants of Lisbon and Oporto, the Archbishop of Braga, and some members of the nobility. A majority of the nobles, however, opted for "legality": that is, they upheld the claims of Queen Beatriz and Juan I.

The claims of another pretender to the throne, a son of Pedro I by Inez de Castro, complicated further an already confused situation. The confusion was somewhat lessened when João of Aviz murdered Andeiro, after which the common people and merchants of Lisbon, urged on by João's supporters, proclaimed him "regent and defender" of the realm.

When Juan I of Castile marched on Portugal to assert his wife's claim, João organized the defense. Though he gained some victories, he was unable to prevent a siege of Lisbon in 1384 which lasted almost five months — and ended only when disease among Juan's troops forced him to abandon the campaign temporarily. With the Spaniards still in the field and perhaps half of Portugal in arms against him, João found sorely needed support in the merchants of the port cities, among a part of the nobility, and in a foreign alliance.[1]

By December 1383, he had already sent a mission to England

to ask Richard II's permission to recruit troops. John of Gaunt's forces had scarcely reached home, having left Portugal with much mutual ill-will after their attempt to claim the Castilian throne for John, but nonetheless Richard assented readily. The idea of helping Portugal appealed to both populace and merchants, and recruits flocked to the standard from all walks of life. London merchants helped finance the expedition, partly, perhaps, because João had sent representatives of the merchants of Lisbon and Oporto along with his own diplomats. Money was also raised by requisitioning Portuguese ships and goods in English waters. The first English troops landed on Portuguese shores four days before João of Aviz was elected João I, King of Portugal, by the national *Côrtes*.

Early in 1385 a *Côrtes* had been called to meet in Coimbra for the purpose of determining who was the realm's legitimate ruler. João's chief legal supporter, the learned João das Regras, "proved" that every claimant to the throne was illegitimate, thereby leaving the election of a ruler in the hands of the *Côrtes*. Thus manipulated, they responded by electing João on April 6, 1385.

On the following August 14, the new king's forces routed an army of Spaniards and foreigners several times their size. The victorious battle of Aljubarrota inaugurated a reign which was, in the beginning, precarious.

II

João I represented more than a change of dynasty: he was the first royal leader of the new bourgeoisie. Although they had been brought to his side by persuasion, the circumstances which caused the merchant class to support João placed him under great obligation to them. They assured his success and he in turn assured theirs. João showed his gratitude and astuteness four days after his election, when he confirmed the charter of the merchants of Lisbon, strengthening some clauses which they desired to protect them against foreign merchants in retail trade. Several additions were made to this legislation during the next few years.

Similarly, João wasted no time in cementing his relations with England. John of Gaunt was disposed to try again for the throne of Castile if the Portuguese would supply the ships to transport his soldiers, and on April 15, 1385, negotiations were opened for a treaty which was concluded May 9, 1386. Although often breached by both parties, this treaty deserves the renown it has achieved. Its political provisions have made it famous as the longest-lived alliance in history. Its economic provisions bound the two nations to numerous mutual concessions and promises of protection to each other's merchants. By a separate agreement, Portugal was to send ten *galés* and maintain them at her own expense to aid Richard II for six months.

The subsequent invasion of Castile was a failure, but the alliance had consequences of lasting importance. In February 1387, João I married Philippa of Lancaster, daughter of John of Gaunt. She became the mother of a king, a saint, and Henry the Navigator. Another of John of Gaunt's daughters married Enrique of Castile, becoming the grandmother of Isabella the Catholic. The eventual union of Spain and Portugal under Philip II of Spain made John of Gaunt's ambitions come true.

There were more immediate consequences of this alliance. The embassies between the countries were frequent. Trade increased; Portuguese merchants and others settled in England; English merchants settled in Portugal; and a number of the ladies of Philippa's suite married there. In 1389, the English merchants received an extension of their privileges based on grants previously made to the Genoese and Piacenzans.[2]

III

The Flemish trade was so regular that only the unusual made news. War was the most frequent cause of irregularities; and the Hundred Years' War often affected normal trade. Another constant problem was the rivalry of England and France in Flanders and the adjacent areas with which the Portuguese regularly traded. But despite such disturbances, the Portuguese *feitoria* functioned as it had done for more than a century past and as it would do for more than a century in the future.

Portugal had no vital interest in the Anglo-French rivalry or in the intercity wars in Italy, but her ubiquitous trade placed her in the middle. She was compelled to keep on the best possible terms with all, but she could not forego an alliance with England to help keep Castile at bay.

The English alliance and the war between England and France made the Channel passage hazardous at times. In order to find an outlet for their goods when the Flemish cities were blocked by war, foreign merchants carried their cargoes to Middelbourg on Walcheren Island, where the alert Albert, Duke of Holland and Zeeland, granted privileges to them. The Portuguese were among such foreign merchants as early as 1384. Two years later we hear of an Italian merchant in England loading his goods on two Portuguese merchants ships bound for Middelbourg. A merchant of Oporto carried a cargo of Valenciennes cloth from Middelbourg to London. Two other merchants, one of them also from Oporto, sent a cargo of skins from London and Sandwich to the same city.

Neither the Count of Flanders nor the citizens of Bruges, who were at war with their count, could ignore the danger such a shift of trade implied. On January 15, 1386, Philip the Bold, Count of Flanders and Duke of Burgundy, granted safe-conducts to the Portuguese on the petition of the merchants of Ypres, Bruges, and Ghent. They were not to call in at English ports either en route to or from Flanders to Portugal. On July 20, 1387, apparently either in response to another appeal or as a clarification of the first grant, Philip gave the Portuguese the same rights enjoyed by other foreign merchants.

Now came the turn of Albert to counter Philip's concessions. To preserve Middelbourg's growing importance, in 1390 he granted to the "merchants, shipmasters, and subjects" of the King of Portugal the right to establish their *feitoria* (*étape*), choose their own consul with powers to settle disputes among themselves, and hold such meetings as they desired. These concessions kept the Portuguese in Middelbourg for some years. They were still trading there in the next century, though their principal center remained in Flanders.

The Portuguese at this time were taking to the northern centers precious stones from the Orient, jewels, pearls, a variety of spices, wines, olives and olive oil, dates, oranges, grapes, almonds, and figs. In exchange they carried away horses, cattle, cheese, butter, codfish and other northern fish, textiles including tapestries, and paintings of the new and flourishing Flemish Renaissance school. We may note that wool from the Iberian Peninsula now began to find a market in Flanders as the English acquired the art of spinning and weaving their own.[3]

IV

Domestic problems were intensified as trade brought more foreigners into Portugal; at the same time, the Portuguese abroad were often in trouble with foreign merchants. The years from 1390 to 1415 were filled with claims and counterclaims. The kings of the various countries were kept busy with the task of protecting their own without driving out the foreigners completely. In 1390, the merchants of Oporto complained to the *Côrtes* of Coimbra that in England and Flanders they were often molested and their goods seized. They wanted João I to seize the properties and bring to court the nationals of those countries trading in Portugal. João ordered his officials to investigate and do vigorous justice to his own subjects as well as to the foreigners.

Portuguese merchants, now richer and stronger, looked with ever more jealousy at the efforts of foreigners to intrude into their domestic trade. In July 1390 there was a repetition of the prohibition against selling foreign goods retail or buying outside specified cities. The exceptions were wine, figs, and salt, which could be bought throughout the country. In February 1391 João again legislated on this subject, but in December he reassured the foreign merchants with a letter of security (*carta de segurança*) to those who had come or might come from enemy territory during the armistice with Castile.

The *de facto* war situation with Castile was no small element in the life of Portugal — and Castile — during these years. Although a three-year armistice had been signed in 1387 and was subsequently renewed for a period of fifteen years, it was not enough to keep the peace. Frequent border raids were the rule. Each side blamed the other, as their historians still do. A merchant of no matter what nationality might find himself in trouble for "trading with the enemy," and suffer loss of property or life. Hence João's letter to give foreign merchants assurance of safety.

He sought to protect them in other ways. In April 1392, Caminha in northern Portugal was designated a free port, the first of which we have a record in Portugal. "All ships whatsoever" were permitted to anchor in a designated area, paying tax only on the part of their cargo landed and sold. In June a similar act was applied to the Venetians, taxing them only on the cargo sold or left behind for sale in Lisbon or elsewhere. In December 1394, the *Côrtes* of Coimbra conferred such privileges on foreign merchants in general, and João warned against molesting foreigners who came to trade.

Portuguese merchants abroad were still having the same troubles. In 1395, a case pending in the Parlement of Paris arose from the arrest of a Portuguese in Amiens and the seizure of a French vessel in reprisal. The English, at about the same time, often seized Portuguese goods for the debts, still unpaid, which João I had incurred in his fight for the throne.

As a result of such troubles, the *companhia das naus* was revived or renewed in 1397. On the petition of the merchants, the King ordered a vote to be taken among them: if a majority voted for the assessments, all must pay. There is no clear indication of the result of the vote, but it seems that the insurance system, of which we heard first in 1293 and again in 1377, was continued in operation. In 1397 also, the Portuguese and Castilians were granted a ten-year exemption from certain taxes in France.

A romantic note in foreign relations was sounded in 1398. Camões, in his *Lusíadas* (canto VI, stanzas 56–68), relates the story of twelve Portuguese gentlemen who went to England to avenge the honor of an equal number of Portuguese ladies who had been outraged there. We must regret that Camões does not record the outcome of the mission.

The more serious matter of maintaining commercial relations in spite of war occupied the attention of the kings. In December 1399, João assured the merchants of Flanders, Brittany, and other regions that they would not be molested in Portugal because of France's war with England, Portugal's ally.

The alliance did not prevent mutual irritations, however, and in this same year Henry IV of England (who had just deposed Richard II) asked his sister, Queen Philippa of Portugal, to intervene with her husband in behalf of English merchants. The result was a series of communications which virtually renewed and rewrote the alliance of 1386, spelling out the rights and privileges of the merchants of each country while trading in the other. Henry IV was better able than Richard II to enforce the protection he promised, but Portuguese merchants were never entirely safe in England, nor English merchants in Portugal.[4]

The records now begin to show as an import of Portugal a product which in past times had more often appeared as an export — wheat and other cereals. Was it the growth of the wine production that made the import of cereals necessary? Or was it the border wars with Spain, which sometimes destroyed crops? Whatever the cause, the effect on Portugal was important. In 1399 and other years, João had no choice but to force his merchants to include in their return cargoes cereals from such regions as England, Flanders, and Brittany. The merchants, of course, preferred the lighter merchandise of greater value. The pressure for access to foods is seen by some writers as a reason for Portuguese expansion, although the regions to which they eventually expanded were not wheat-growing.

The pattern of mutual concessions and settlement of grievances was so well established that they are mentioned only to show the advanced stage of development of Portugal's overseas contacts at this time. Portuguese merchants joined with English merchants to import wheat, arms, and other products into Portugal. Italian merchants living in England and Portugal also participated.⁵ Both Italians and English enjoyed the well-known privileges of trade, João I in 1400 specifically granting to the English privileges based on those enjoyed by the Genoese.

If treaties could have ended the quarrels of the merchants, there would have been few difficulties. But there was a basic conflict which could hardly be settled by royal agreements. The merchants of Portugal and of other countries were now rich and aggressive; they wanted to keep the commerce at home in their own hands while retaining privileges abroad. So it is no wonder that the ink on the parchment was barely sanded before fresh complaints arrived. The early years of the fifteenth century found the chancelleries almost constantly engaged in preparing either new agreements and promises of protection or excuses for their own merchants and complaints against those of other countries. From these documents we can safely draw one conclusion: the profits of commerce were very high or the merchants could not have sustained the losses they inflicted on one another. Citing the dates only, we find that in 1400, 1401, 1403, 1404, and 1405 João made complaints about the treatment of his merchants abroad while issuing laws regulating the transactions of foreigners or granting them charters in his own country.

In order to lessen the friction between their two countries, the English and Portuguese tried to put a bit more cement into their alliance in 1405 by the marriage of Beatriz, illegitimate daughter of João I, to Thomas, Count of Arundel, who was granted a dowry of 6250 marks of silver by João.

Much of the trade and many of the ships now belonged to João. From the time of Afonso Henriques, as we have seen, there had developed a tradition of the crown carrying on business in its own right. Thus in the year 1405 João sent his own ships to regions as far separated as Norway, Flanders, and Genoa. The king as business man was nothing new in Portugal; nor was the royal family less given to business in the centuries that lay ahead.⁶

It has long since been made clear that the ramifications of Portuguese trade had reached all parts of western Europe and included the Mediterranean. From the early years of the fifteenth century, there were Portuguese vessels (as well as Basque, English, Dutch, and others) in the Balearic Islands and other ports of the Mediterranean, and their number increased as the century progressed. Their cargoes were often wheat, brought from the northern countries. The Portuguese were thus definitely a connecting link between the Mediterranean and the North Sea.

They were still active in Middelbourg in 1407. At the same time their *feitoria* in Bruges remained the principal center of their Flemish trade. Here, in 1410, the Prior of San Domingos monastery granted the merchants of Portugal and Algarve the chapel of Santa Cruz, which was to serve as a burial ground for the exclusive use of the Portuguese, or those they permitted to lie alongside. Flemish merchants in Lisbon were granted similar rights by the friars of San Domingos, not later than 1414.

Shipbuilding and the stimulation of commerce were the constant aim of João I. In 1410, he granted a new charter to Oporto providing that the goods of "Castile, Biscay, and Galicia from Fuenterrabía to the River Minho," by whatever merchants brought, were exempt from the tithe except on certain listed goods. These included gold, silver, iron, steel, lead, and some textiles. He also provided for a species of subsidy to shipbuilding. Materials imported for shipbuilding or repairing of ships as specified in a list would receive a rebate of the tithe if the ship was begun or repaired within one year. In 1410, João also issued price lists applying to both Lisbon and Oporto, which show a large variety of goods from all parts of Europe.

In 1411, peace was finally established with Spain, leaving free Portuguese energies which had been held in check by the border hostilities. In Flanders, Portugal's position was strengthened when John the Fearless, Duke of Burgundy, issued to the Portuguese merchants a charter of *liberdades e privilégios*. The next year temporary difficulties caused an interruption in trade with both Flanders and France, but such misunderstandings were usual and there was but a brief break in relations. Count

William of Holland seized the moment to renew the privileges of the Portuguese and others trading with his realms. In 1413, Henry V of England reaffirmed the famed *carta mercatoria* of 1303.[7]

João I was never a man of short vision. From the moment he so opportunely seized a throne that was not his, he had shown great capacities as planner and doer. He was already planning the most significant move of his reign — perhaps the most significant move in the life of his nation — the invasion of Africa.[8]

Chapter Nine

Time for Conquest

Three feverish years of preparation preceded the eve of Ceuta.[1] Three centuries of expanding shipping and commerce had gone before. Portuguese trade now reached all Europe, and Portuguese merchants ranked high in affairs of state.

João I had ever shown a disposition to honor the obligations to his people incurred on his ascent to the throne. Now a nationalistic rich shipping class was prepared to repay the King in loyalty and money. This fruitful partnership of merchants and monarch did not stand alone. João had neglected neither the landed nobles nor the gentry, and they would not fail him. Being based on both commerce and agriculture, Portugal was neither solely an agrarian nor a commercial kingdom. Because the bulk of her commerce had always been drawn from the products of her soil, the interests of farmer and merchant were united into one common, national concern.

Solid, conservative, gradual are the words to describe Portugal's commercial progress to 1415. True, there had been adventures into the unknown Atlantic during the fourteenth century, but the seafaring activities of Portugal to this date were primarily commercial rather than adventurous. The men who shipped into and from the ports of Portugal were following the well-sailed routes where charters of "privileges and liberties" made them welcome. João of Aviz, looking to the well-being of his subjects, had preferred to exploit old routes rather than explore the uncharted Atlantic. There had been enough to do in maintaining independence from Spain; in keeping open the channels of commerce with Italy and France, England, and Flanders; in becoming merchants and sailors who were the peers of any in Europe. This had been achievement enough for the generation that was young in 1383. They were old men

now; and they had just seen the consummation of their life-
long struggle in the peace treaty of 1411. The merchants had
what they wanted in the favorable trade agreements. The older
generation, João I among them, might have been content to let
things go on as before.

Lisbon and Oporto were cosmopolitan ports where every
manner of men and every tongue found common speech in
pursuit of profit. No other state of Europe welcomed foreigners
so heartily as did Portugal; no other granted them so many
privileges; no other profited so much from the assimilation of
foreign talents. The kings of Portugal asked only that the
foreigner be useful to the nation; and in return, privileges
awaited. From diversity had come unity and strength.

Such was the situation when João decided to launch his
forces to attack the continent of Africa. Why did he make such
a decision? What were his motives? What were his means? We
can arrive at an approximate answer to the latter question with
no great difficulty. But when it comes to motives we are faced
with the many and varied choices which have confronted historians from the time of Azurara, the official chronicler of the
conquest of Ceuta, to the present moment. While we could
point out any number, each of which might have been the true
motive, a combination, not one alone, seems a more satisfactory
and reasonable answer.

II

In 1412, João had three sons of an age to take part in affairs
of state. The scholarly Duarte was to become king and die in
his mid-forties after a brief reign. Pedro was to live strenuously,
rule Portugal as regent, and die tragically in civil war. Henry
was to become the Navigator, patron of voyagers and explorers.
For Duarte a throne was waiting, but to Pedro and Henry the
world offered only opportunity. Too vigorous and intelligent
to be contained in narrow confines, Pedro traveled widely and
served foreign princes, including the Holy Roman Emperor.
Henry, perhaps even before Ceuta, projected his mind into the
unknown Atlantic and African worlds. But Pedro's travels and
Henry's oceanic concerns lay in the future. In 1412, they were

casting about for a task worthy of their talents and ambitions. Henry was only eighteen when preparations for Ceuta began, Pedro a year older. But Henry was in charge of mobilizing the men and resources of the northern part of Portugal, and Pedro had the same responsibility in the south. Both did well.

Some historians would have it that at this point such a relatively minor matter as the winning of a knighthood played a major role. Azurara says that the princes had persuaded their father to invite French knights to a tourney in order to try their skill; and it is certain that the French knights were in Portugal. However, others hold that their desire to win knighthood on the field of battle inspired Pedro and Henry to urge the African campaign on their father — a natural ambition for youths of their age.

Pedro and Henry might be considered representative of Portugal's dominant class of their time. Backing up these young royal sons were hundreds of others from the nobility: as Fernão Lopes wrote, "Another, new world arose, and a new generation of men." There was energy to spare in Portugal. The question was not *if* it would burst out, but when and where. The thirty years since Aljubarrota had satisfied the older men, but their sons had had little taste of the booty of war. Many in Portugal, and not all of them the youngsters, would have renewed the war with Spain in order to take advantage of the turmoil under the infant king, Juan II. "There was a great opportunity," Azurara remarks, "for us to sally into that kingdom, from the robbery of which we would enrich our whole country."

Such sentiments appealed to the class that would enjoy the spoils, which is not to say all those who would do the fighting. Most of the commoners, even many of the rich merchants, would bear the burdens of war without its rewards. Peace with Spain served them best. Azurara also speaks for them: "Henceforth we shall be able to enjoy our goods and sell our products without fear or hindrance; now our merchants will be able to travel safely throughout all Spain and sell their merchandise." João I, more in accord with this view of the merchants than that of those who would make war on Spain, rejected any thought of breaking the recently signed treaty.

Far better to make war on the infidel, so João proposed to Castile a joint attack on Granada. But weak or strong, Castile wanted no rival conqueror in Granada. That was to be a Castilian enterprise when the day came. She refused the Portuguese offer; and João turned to Africa.

III

Africa was not a new thought to Portugal, or to Castile, or to Aragon.[2] Long before the Reconquest was completed, the Christian states had laid down lines of demarcation in their advance into Moslem territory. At first such lines were in the Peninsula — divisions between Castile and Portugal, between Castile and Aragon, divisions of lands to be conquered.

Castilian-Aragonese agreements dated back to the twelfth century, at a time when they were still on the defensive against the Moslems. Once they were definitely advancing, they looked to a distant future and divided Africa between them. In 1291, Jaime II of Aragon and Sancho IV of Castile signed the Convention of Soria which set the demarcation line of the conquest-to-come at the Muluya River, Aragon receiving rights of conquest eastward where she already had claimed a protectorate since 1280, and Castile westward from the Muluya to the Atlantic.

The year 1291 was the date of the Genoese Vivaldi expedition; early in the next century came other Genoese voyages and the naming of some of the Canaries. In the fourteenth century, as we have seen, Portugal protested against the Castilian claims in the Canaries.

Africa was not a consideration in the Castilian-Portuguese wars prior to the fifteenth century, but given the success of both peoples against the Moslems, the eventual conflict became certain. Also, contrary to the treaty of 1291, both Catalan and Mallorcan sailors visited the west coast of Africa and the Canaries during the course of the fourteenth century. In 1393, a Castilian expedition of considerable force visited the Canaries, bringing back slaves. With the object of striking a blow against the North African Moslems, Enrique III of Castile in 1400 sent a force which raided the coast, capturing and sacking Tetuán, a center of trade and piratical forays.[3] Other expeditions served to accentuate the arrival of Castile on the Atlantic as an aggressive maritime power before 1402, when Jean de Bethencourt, and Gadifer de la Salle, with the authorization of Enrique III of Castile, made the first permanent European settlement in the Canaries, giving Castile a definite title. When the peace treaty between Spain and Portugal was signed in 1411, Portugal was about to be cut off from Africa and — if Castilian expansion went unchallenged — perhaps from African Atlantic trade. The refusal of Castile to join in a war against Moslem Granada left Portugal free to prepare her thrust into Africa.

Thus it can be seen that matters far weightier than knighthood for three doughty sons persuaded João I to embark on an ambitious overseas policy. That he long pondered the African invasion and reached a decision only after taking counsel with his court is well attested by the chroniclers. It was not a move to be undertaken lightly. He would encounter the strength of the Moslems and dare the hostility of Castile, which never ceased to be a threat no matter how many treaties were signed.

IV

Three years of intensive activity followed João's final decision. Never before had Portugal prepared for an enterprise of this magnitude. This was no border raid on Castile, but an overseas expedition against a strongly fortified place in the hands of a numerous and brave enemy. "Many ships, many men, much money" were needed. In fact, hundreds of ships, thousands of men, and hitherto unthought-of quantities of money.

Money was difficult to come by. Portugal was short of gold and silver; all Europe was short of gold and silver. The desire to tap the African source, to get behind the Moslems to the gold producers instead of having to obtain coins from the Moslems through trade, was one of the strongest motivations for the great venture. Eventually it was to pay off, but meanwhile João had to borrow money or manufacture it. The minters were feverishly busy. "Night and day," says Azurara, "their hammers were never quiet" as new coins were cut from base metals which João's fiat converted into gold and silver. The result of the policy was a pre-credit type of inflation; but it served its immediate purpose: "much money" was provided.

Most of the ships and most of the men could be supplied by Portugal, but she could not yet muster a fleet of the extraordinary proportions for the great adventure. However, past experience served her well in making up the deficit. Portugal had contacts in every port in western Europe. She could and did call on Galicia, Biscay, Brittany, France, England, and Flanders for ships.

Various types of Portuguese vessels were ready for the expedition. The galley (*galé,* later called *galera*) had developed greatly since 1317 when Admiral Peçanha had come from Genoa. All Europe admired these Portuguese galleys, some of which, by João I's time, were propelled by three hundred rowers. In contrast to the galley, which might be ten times as long as it was wide, the *nau* was only twice as long as wide. Slow and awkward, its bulk was capable of carrying a much larger cargo and more men with fewer sailors than the galley required. Smaller, but agile and useful, were the *barcha* and the *barinel,* sailing ships of only twenty-five or thirty tons, yet capable of braving the high seas as carriers of cargo, men, or messengers. These were the predecessors of the famous caravel, which succeeded them after 1441 as the ships of exploration sent out by Henry, and which later bore Columbus to America and Da Gama to India. Would these ships have been available, whether borrowed or home-built, without Portugal's long maritime history?[4]

If the money and the ships were problems, the men were not. The nation's fervent enthusiasm for the undertaking generated scenes in which men of ninety presented themselves in sword and buckler to the youthful Henry. Recruits flocked from all parts of Europe — England, France, Germany, Poland. Doubtless more ships, money, and men would have been drawn from England and France but for the fact that in the summer of

1415 Henry V of England was leading his men against the French in the campaign which would culminate in the October victory at Agincourt. Nevertheless, at the request of the Council of Lisbon the English monarch permitted the export in 1414–1415 of lances and other arms to Portugal.

An uneasiness spread over European courts with the news of the vast preparations. What were João's intentions? Such activities could not be kept secret with hundreds of foreign ships and thousands of sailors touching Portugal during those years. But the objective of attack was not revealed. The kings of Castile and Aragon sent embassies of inquiry, and received assurances of friendship. To the Duke of Holland, João sent open defiance on the pretext of a recent commercial disagreement, but secretly the Duke was reassured. The ruler of Granada complained that his merchants were now afraid to go to Portugal as they had been accustomed to do from distant times past. João gave no assurance to this embassy and invoked the laws against trading with the infidel.[5]

By July 1415, preparations for the venture were complete. All was in readiness: the men, the ships, the money, and the Portuguese nation. But the auguries were unfavorable. When plague broke out and Queen Philippa died, the weak of spirit saw omens and doubted. But they were not truly of the "new generation of men." The fleet sailed, and Ceuta fell on August 21 after only one day of furious battle.

Portugal was now launched on the imperial road from which there was no point of voluntary return. The precarious beach-head on the rim of the endless Moslem world could not be abandoned without loss of prestige and self-respect. The hope for profit, the conquest of souls, the cutting off of Castile, were now identified with Portugal's national spirit. Her mission was to seek out the infidel wherever he was, to convert him, to seize his territory, to circumvent his commerce, and eventually, as Henry would see it, to find a waterway to the Indies.

To Henry, history has justly awarded the honor of exploring the road that began in Ceuta. None would or could deprive him of the praise his career invokes. But back of Henry stretched those centuries which made his work possible. Without the accumulation of maritime and commercial experience, without the unified monarchy, without Portuguese national spirit, there could have been no Navigator. Those who agree with Adam Smith that the greatest events of human history were the discoveries of Columbus and Da Gama must surely agree that they could not have sailed if there had been no Henry. His is a name with which we evoke three centuries of preparation for the three centuries of the Great Explorations.[6]

NOTES

If all the sources bearing on the subject of Portuguese overseas contacts before the capture of Ceuta were given here, the size of the book would be increased several times without adding anything essential. The author has examined substantially every work related to the subject and has carefully verified references to documents and works that may be considered sources. Such works in accessible books and articles will be cited, but will not be, or may not be, named again after the first citation unless they contain material which amplifies or contradicts the point under discussion.

CHAPTER ONE

1 August 21 is now the accepted date for the capture of Ceuta. Some authors formerly gave August 15 to lend a religious significance to the expedition. See Edgar Prestage, *The Portuguese Pioneers* (London, 1933), pp. 23-25. But Fortunato de Almeida, *História de Portugal* (6 vols., Coimbra, 1922-1929), pp. 23-38, and the works he cites, show the date as August 21. Hereafter cited as Almeida, *História Portugal*. Portuguese motives for the Ceuta attack are discussed in the last chapter of this book.

2 A standard and excellent work on Portuguese expansion is that of António Baião, Hernani Cidade, and Manuel Múrias, *História da expansão portuguesa no mundo* (3 vols., Lisbon, 1937-1940). It is an authoritative, cooperative work by the leading scholars of Portugal. Hereafter cited as *História expansão portuguesa*. The standard modern history is Damião Peres (ed.), *História de Portugal: Edição Monumental* (8 vols., Barcelos, 1928-1938). Hereafter cited as *História Portugal Monumental*. Volume I carries down to the *Condado Portucalense*.

3 The most complete work on the Portuguese world in all its aspects is the *Congresso do mundo português: Publicações* (19 vols., Lisbon, 1940). Hereafter cited as *Mundo português*. Volume I covers prehistory. All the above have bibliographies. See also *A Catalog of The William B. Greenlee Collection of Portuguese History and Literature and the Portuguese Materials in The Newberry Library*, compiled by Doris Varner Welsh (Chicago, 1953); and Bernard Xavier C. Coutinho, *Bibliographie Franco-Portugaise*, Institut Français au Portugal (Oporto, 1939).

4 Early history and much of the medieval history pertinent to this study are treated by L. Saavedra Machado in "Os ingleses em Portugal," published in *Biblos: Revista da Faculdade de Letras da Universidade de Coimbra*, be-

ginning in volume VIII, 1932, and running through to XIII, 1937. Hereafter cited as Saavedra Machado, in *Biblos*.

5 Saavedra Machado, in *Biblos*, VIII, 469-479.

6 *Ibid.*, VIII, 479-496.

7 The statement that there were Portuguese at Le Landit is based on Jules
Thieury, *Le Portugal et la Normandie jusqu'à la fin du XVI*e *siècle* (Paris,
1860), p. 3, who holds that Spaniards means also Portuguese. Saavedra Machado, in *Biblos*, VIII, 496, uses Émile Levasseur, *Histoire du commerce de
la France* (Paris, 1911), I, 36, who says only that among the merchants were
some from Spain. See also Manuel Colmeiro, *Historia de la economía en
España* (2 vols., Madrid, 1863), I, 136-145. Hereafter cited as Colmeiro,
Historia España.

8 Saavedra Machado, in *Biblos*, VIII, 497-498; Colmeiro, *Historia España*, I,
196-202.

9 Luis Montalvor (ed.), *História do régimen republicano em Portugal* (2
vols., Lisbon, 1930), I, 37-40, gives a very favorable view of Arabic influence.
Hereafter cited as Montalvor, *Régimen republicano*. There is a tendency by
some recent writers to belittle Arabic civilization. Louis Bertrand, *Histoire
d'Espagne* (Paris, 1932), pp. 23-63 and 122-138, presents an anti-Arab view.
Henri Pirenne holds the Arabs rather than the barbarian invaders to blame
for the decline of commerce in western Europe. There is no justification for
this view with regard to Spain and Portugal, if there is anywhere. See
Henri Pirenne, *Histoire de l'Europe des invasions au XVI*e *siècle* (8th ed.,
Paris-Brussels, 1936), pp. 18-24, and also his *Medieval Cities: Their Origins
and the Revival of Trade* (Princeton, 1925), pp. 1-24. A more recent view
is found in Évariste Lévi-Provençal, *La civilisation arabe en Espagne* (Paris,
1948), and other works by the same author.

10 The usual works cited on this point are listed in an accessible Portuguese
history by António Gonçalves Mattoso, *História de Portugal* (2 vols., Lisbon,
1939), I, 3-16.

11 There are numerous works on the Vikings. For a bibliography see Herbert
Heaton, *Economic History of Europe* (New York, 1948), pp. 84-85, or, for
fuller reference, M. Postan and E. E. Rich (eds.), *The Cambridge Economic
History of Europe* (Cambridge, 1952), II, chapter IV and the bibliography,
pp. 531-536. A standard work is Charles H. Haskins, *The Normans in
European History* (Boston and New York, 1915).

12 Saavedra Machado, in *Biblos*, VIII, 499.

13 Jaime Cortesão, in Montalvor, *Régimen republicano*, I, 39, holds that such
words as *barca, quilha, mastro,* and perhaps *leme* were introduced to Portugal by the Vikings. If so, the Vikings must have taken them from Latin. On
Charlemagne see Émile Vandenbussche, *Flandre et Portugal: mémoire sur
les relations qui existèrent autrefois entre les flammands de Flandre — par-
ticulièrement ceux de Bruges — et les portugais* (Bruges, 1874), pp. 17-18.
Cited hereafter as Vandenbussche, *Flandre-Portugal*. Other material is found
in the review *La Flandre,* which Vandenbussche edited.

14 The chronology of the Vikings is too sketchy to permit exact dating. See L. Saavedra Machado, *Expedições normandas no ocidente da Hispania,* Instituto Alemão da Universidade de Coimbra (Coimbra, 1931), pp. 3-6, and the numerous references given there. See also Charles de la Roncière, *Histoire de la marine française* (6 vols., Paris, 1899-1934), I, 93-111. All subsequent authors cite Reinhart P. A. Dozy, *Histoire des musulmans d'Espagne,* of which there is a new edition by É. Lévi-Provençal (3 vols., Leyden, 1932). The basic collection of sources is by Henrique Flórez, Manuel Risco, and others (eds.), *España sagrada* (51 vols., 1754-1859), a compilation of medieval chronicles. The authenticity of this collection, frequently criticized for its alleged inaccuracies, could have been verified only by direct consultation of the manuscripts from which it was taken, each of which would require collation with all known copies. Some checking has been done, and we must rest here on Saavedra Machado's reading. See other information in *Biblos,* IX, 139-154, 378-395.

15 Saavedra Machado, *Expedições normandas,* pp. 4-24, uses Émile Levasseur, *Commerce de la France,* I, 32, and one of the basic collections of Portuguese documents, Alexandre Herculano and others (eds.), *Portugaliae monumenta histórica* (21 fascicles, usually in 7 vols., Lisbon, 1856-1936), *Diplomata et chartae,* I, 61. Hereafter cited as *P.M.H.* Other important documents are in *Vimaranis monumenta histórica* (2 parts, Guimarães, 1908, I, 14-15. See also Reinhart P. A. Dozy, *Recherches sur l'histoire et la littérature en Espagne pendent le Moyen Âge* (2 vols., Paris, 1881 and other editions), II, 250-350; La Roncière, *Marine française,* I, 104-111; Manuel Gomez de Lima Bezerra, *Os estranjeiros no Lima* (2 vols., Coimbra, 1785-1791), I, 133 *et seq., passim;* Joaquim de Santa Rosa Viterbo, *Elucidário das palavras, termos, e frases que em Portugal antiguamente se usárão* (2 vols., 1st ed., Lisbon, 1798; 2nd ed., Lisbon, 1865), see the word *Laudomanes,* hereafter cited as Viterbo, *Elucidário;* É. Cantineau, "Origines des relations commerciales entre la Flandre et le Portugal," in *Boletim da Sociedade de Geografia de Lisboa,* series XVIII, no. 1. Hereafter cited as Cantineau, *Flandre-Portugal.* Do not expect to find close agreement as to dates among these works. Even some of the chronicles in *España sagrada* give varying dates for what seem to be the same expeditions. Often an interpretation depends on one word, or a few words, in a Latin manuscript, which may be different in the different copies of the manuscript.

16 The principal, though not uncontroversial, facts concerning the Normans in the Mediterranean may be found in Haskins, *Normans,* pp. 192-249, or any standard medieval history. Two excellent brief treatments of the history of Portugal are Charles E. Nowell, *A History of Portugal* (New York, 1952), and H. V. Livermore, *A History of Portugal* (Cambridge, England, 1947).

CHAPTER TWO

1 Petit de Vausse, "Croisades bourguignonnes," in *Revue Historique,* XXX (1886), 259-269, takes his material largely from the chronicles of the time.

2 L. Vieira de Castro, *A formação de Portugal* (Lisbon, 1938), pp. 13 ff.; see also Frei António Brandão, *Crónica do Conde D. Henrique, D. Teresa e*

Infante D. Afonso, ed. by A. Magalhães Basto (Oporto, 1944); A. Gonçalves Pereira, "Les relations économiques franco-portugais," in *Bulletin des Études Portugaises* (Lisbon, 1939), fascicle 11, which presents the view that Abbot Hugh of Cluny might have sought to establish an independent Portugal to prevent the growth of Castilian power; Vandenbussche, *Flandre-Portugal,* pp. 18-19; Alexandre Herculano, *Opúsculos* (3rd ed., 10 vols., Lisbon, 1907-1908), VI, 30-42, admits the possibility that foreign rivalries helped Portugal but prefers to think that internal strength explains Portuguese national survival. On this point see also Ramón Menéndez Pidal, *La España del Cid* (2 vols., Madrid, 1929), I, 61-62; Damião Peres, *Como nasceu Portugal* (2nd ed., Oporto, 1942); A. A. Mendes Corrêa, *As raizes de Portugal* (2nd ed., Lisbon, 1944); and *Mundo português,* II, which contains a number of articles pertinent to this question.

3 Almeida, *História Portugal,* I, 129-132, cites numerous sources for the period of Count Henrique; see also Petit de Vausse, "Croisades bourguignonnes," in *Revue Historique,* XXX, 269 ff.

4 Vandenbussche, *Flandre-Portugal,* p. 27. The pertinent Flemish history can be found in Ernest van Bruyssel, *Histoire du commerce et de la marine en Belgique* (3 vols., Brussels, 1861-1865), I, *passim;* Henri Pirenne, *Histoire de Belgique* (7 vols., Brussels, 1900-1932), I, *passim;* Henri Pirenne, *Bibliographie de l'histoire de Belgique* (3rd ed., Brussels, 1931); Joseph M. B. C. Kervyn de Lettenhove, *Histoire de la Flandre* (6 vols., Brussels, 1847-1850); also Kervyn de Lettenhove, *Chroniques relatives à l'histoire de la Belgique sous la domination des ducs de Bourgogne* (3 vols., Brussels, 1870-1876); Leopold August Warnkoenig, *Histoire de la Flandre et de ses institutions civiles et politiques, jusqu'à l'année 1305,* translated with additions and omissions by A. Gheldolf (5 vols., Brussels, 1835-1864). Much early Flemish history is taken from Jaques de Meyer, *Commentarii sive annales rerum flandricarum* (Bruges, 1531, Antwerp, 1561, and other printings), which is used as a source for later writings.

The corresponding Portuguese development of fairs and markets, and their tie with Flanders and other northern regions, is treated in Virginia Rau, *Subsídios para o estudo das feiras medievais portuguesas* (Lisbon, 1943); and in Anselmo Braamcamp Freire, *Maria Brandoa (A do Crisfal): A feitoria de Flandres,* first published in the *Archivo Histórico Portuguez,* VI-VIII (11 vols., Lisbon, 1903-1917), and later reprinted as a separate volume with some additions (Lisbon, 1921). The *Archivo Histórico Portuguez* published a great number of valuable documents and is sometimes mistakenly cited as if it were an archive. Hereafter, *A.H.P.*

5 Henrique da Gama Barros, *História da administração pública em Portugal nos séculos XII-XV,* ed. Torquato de Sousa Soares (2nd ed., 12 vols., Lisbon, 1945-1960), IX, 317-318. This work, first published 1885-1922, is one of the classic works of Portuguese scholarship. It is based on thorough archival research and extensive secondary works. The title is somewhat deceptive, concealing the abundant economic and social material contained therein. Hereafter cited as *Administração pública.* The extensive bibliographies in the second edition of Gama Barros contain the fundamental references for the history of Portugal.

6 Saavedra Machado, *Expedições normandas*, pp. 16-19; Dozy, *Recherches*, II, 316 ff.; Almeida, *História Portugal*, I, 401; Cantineau, *Flandre-Portugal*, p. 17; and the following works by Jules Finot: *Étude historique sur les relations commerciales entre la Flandre et l'Espagne, Extrait des Annales du Comité Flamand de France* (Paris, 1899), hereafter cited as *Flandre-Espagne;* and *Étude historique sur les relations commerciales entre la Flandre et la République de Gênes au Moyen Âge* (Paris, 1906), hereafter cited as *Flandre-Gênes;* and *Étude historique sur les relations commerciales entre la France et la Flandre au Moyen Âge* (Paris, 1894), hereafter cited as *France-Flandre.*

7 Rau, *Feiras medievais portuguesas,* pp. 39 ff.

8 Montalvor, *Régimen republicano,* I, 22-23, 43-49, 62-64; Gama Barros, *Administração pública,* IX, 278, 285, 325, X, 207-220, 313-314, 333. Also see two other essential works for the period: Alberto Sampaio, *Estudos históricos e económicos* (2 vols., Oporto, 1923), I, an excellent history of the early maritime relations of the north of Portugal; and A. de Sousa Silva Costa Lobo, *História da sociedade em Portugal no século XV* (Lisbon, 1904), which contains materials for the period prior to the fifteenth century.

9 R. Francisque-Michel, *Les Portugais en France, Les Français en Portugal* (Paris, 1882). Hereafter cited as Michel, *Portugais-Français*. Francisque-Michel is catalogued under Michel in United States libraries. See also Cantineau, *Flandre-Portugal,* pp. 15-16.

10 Roberto S. Lopez, *Genova marinara nel duecento* (Milan, 1933), pp. 163, 177 n. 9; Gama Barros, *Administração pública,* IX, 321-322. Lopez is among those who record that in 1133 Bishop Diego Gelmirez of Compostella sent to Genoa, Pisa, and Arles for shipbuilders, and that only Genoa responded, sending one expert. The source for this information is the *Historia compostellana,* in *España sagrada,* XX, bk. I, ch. 103. Vitorino Magalhães Godinho, *Les grandes découvertes,* offprint from *Bulletin des Études Portugaises* (Coimbra, 1953), gives 1120 and says two ships were built which cleaned out the Moslems from the Galician shores. But, he says, the ocean-going type of ship developed from the Cantabrian *coque,* or *coca,* which was imitated by others, that the Italians taught the Spaniards and Portuguese only how to build the Mediterranean type vessels for commerce and for war, but did not contribute the ships that were later used in the Atlantic. Guido Po, *La marina italiana in Portogallo,* in *Mundo português,* III, 655 ff., has it that the Genoese constructed *buon numero* of *galés* in Galicia and that the Genoese ships were already carrying on an active trade with Portugal and the Atlantic coast of Spain. See also Guido Po in Luigi Federzoni (ed.), *Relazione storiche fra l'Italia e il Portogallo, Memorie e Documenti* (Academia Reale d'Italia, Rome, 1940), pp. 261-322.

11 For a bibliography of the interesting and at times embittered controversy raging around the battle of Ourique, see Almeida, *História Portugal,* I, 142-144; and on the early period in general see Frei António Brandão, *Crónica de D. Afonso Henriques,* ed. A. Magalhães Basto (Oporto, 1945), and Basto (ed.), *Crónica de cinco reyes* (Oporto, 1945).

12 Fortunato de Almeida, *História da Igreja em Portugal* (4 vols. in 8 tomes, Coimbra, 1910-1922), I, 165-173; P. Miguel de Oliveira, "Origins da ordem de Cister em Portugal," in *Revista Portuguesa de História*, V (1951), 317-355. The latest authoritative work on papal relations is Carl Erdman, *O papado e Portugal no primeiro século da história portuguesa*, offprint from *Boletim do Instituto Alemão*, V (Coimbra, 1935).

13 Saavedra Machado, *Expedições normandas*, pp. 19-21, and also in *Biblos*, X, 38-39. The classical work for the history of Portugal to 1278 is Alexandre Herculano, *História de Portugal*, ed. David Lopes (8th ed., Lisbon, n.d. [1908-1914 ?]), II, 200-223, 309-311.

14 Almeida, *História Portugal*, I, 168; Federzone (ed.), *Relazione Italia-Portogallo*, pp. 87-89.

15 The basic document on the capture of Santarém in 1147 is *De expugnatione scalabis*, in *P.M.H., Scriptores*, I, 94-95, used by Almeida, *História Portugal*, I, 150-157, Herculano, *Historia Portugal*, II, 217 ff. See also António Brandão and Bernardo de Brito, *Monarchia lusitana* (8 vols., 1597 and later printings), bk. X, chs. xxii, xxiii, xxiv. This work must be cited in books and chapters because of the confusion in identifying pages in the various printings. Other material is in Visconde de Santarém and L. A. Rebêlo da Silva, *Quadro elementar das relações politicas e diplomáticas de Portugal com as diversas potências do mundo* (19 vols., Paris-Lisbon, 1842-1876), XIV, *passim*. Hereafter cited as *Quadro elementar*. The reader should note two things about this fundamental collection of documents: first, unfortunately, it is not always reliable and should be checked against other material when possible; second, dates are given in both Era of Caesar and Era of Christ, but the distinction is not always made clear and is sometimes obviously erroneous. All dating in Portugal prior to 1422 was Era of Caesar, which began 38 years before the Christian era. Therefore, subtract 38 years to find the Christian date. For example, a date given as 1438 Era is A.D. 1400.

The basic document for the conquest of Lisbon is Charles Wendell David (ed.), *The Conquest of Lisbon* (New York, 1936), a translation and study of *De expugnatione lyxbonense*, written by a participant in the conquest. Secondary accounts are found in all the standard histories, Almeida, Herculano, Peres, and in Saavedra Machado, in *Biblos*, IX, 553-566, X, 37 ff., 573 ff.

16 Almeida, *História Portugal*, I, 157-162, with bibliography; Saavedra Machado, as cited in note 15 above; Montalvor, *Régimen republicano*, I, 55; *Monarchia lusitana*, bk. X, chs. xxv ff.; A. de Veiga Simões, *La Flandre, le Portugal et les débuts du capitalisme moderne*, offprint from *Revue Économique Internationale* (Brussels, 1932); Herculano, *História Portugal*, III, 54 ff.; Braamcamp Freire, *A Feitoria*, pp. 33 ff.; *Quadro elementar*, III, 2-3.

17 How much trade during these years? And how much carried by crusaders? Many historians have emphasized the stimulus given by the crusades to the trade of such cities as Lisbon and Oporto which served as stopping and provisioning points between southern and northern Europe. Among others see Thieury. *Portugal-Normandie;* Veiga Simões, *Flandre-Portugal;* and

Michel, *Portugal-France*. Recently, however, R. Doehaerd, *Les relations commerciales entre Gênes, la Belgique et l'outrement d'après les archives notariales génoises aux XIIIᵉ et XIVᵉ siècles* (3 vols., Brussels-Rome, 1941), II, 84 ff., insists that no trade whatever was done by the crusaders. Hereafter cited as Doehaerd, *Gênes-Belgique*.

18 Gama Barros, *Administração pública*, IX, 316-317, cites Wilhelm von Heyd, *Histoire du commerce du Levant au Moyen Âge* (2 vols., 1885), I, 244, n. 5, and 264. Hereafter cited as Heyd, *Commerce-Levant*. Heyd's reference is to Timarion's chronicle, edited in Paris by M. Hase, in *Notices et extraits de manuscrits de la Bibliothèque Nationale, Institut de France, Academie des Inscriptions et Belles Lettres* (Paris, 1813), IX, part 2, p. 171. Timarion used the word "Lusitanian" which indicates he meant Christians. The manuscript of this chronicle is now back in the Vatican from which Napoleon took it during his invasion of Italy.

CHAPTER THREE

1 Heaton, *Economic Europe*, pp. 86-88, 154-166; Hilmar C. Krueger, "Genoese Trade with Northwest Africa," in *Speculum*, VIII (1933), 377-395; Finot, *Flandre-Gênes*, pp. 1-5; Michele G. Canale, *Degli antichi navigatori genovesi* (Genoa, 1846), pp. 1-9; Michele G. Canali, *Nuova istoria della republica di Genova* (4 vols., Florence, 1858-1864), I, 304, 326-327; Rafael Altamira, *Historia de España* (4 vols., Madrid, 1904-1913), I, 402-404.

2 Gama Barros, *Administração pública*, X, 317-318; Montalvor, *Régimen republicano*, I, 51-54. The classical work on Christian trade with the Moslems is M. L. de Mas Latrie, *Traités de paix et de commerce et documents divers concernants les relations chrétiens avec les Arabes de l'Afrique septentrionale au Moyen Âge* (Paris, 1866-1872), and other works by the same author. See *Quadro elementar*, I, 95, on Christian-Moslem trade in Portugal.

3 Benjamin de Tudela has been cited to justify the statement that the Portuguese (i.e., Christians) were trading in Montpellier in 1166. What Benjamin says does not entirely rule out the possibility that Moslems (or even Portuguese Christians) were in Montpellier and Marseilles, but such a conclusion is based on inference rather than hard fact. He says: "Men come for business there [Montpellier] from all quarters, from Edom, Ismael, the land of Algarve [?], Lombardy, the dominions of Rome the Great, from all the lands of Egypt, Palestine, Greece, France, Asia and England. People of all nations are found there doing business through the medium of Genoese and Pisans." *Itinerary of Benjamin of Tudela*, tr. and ed. Marcus Nathan Adler (London, 1907), pp. 3 ff. *passim*. A translation made by Asher in 1840 inserted "Portugal" after the word translated as "Algarve." A comparison of various Hebrew texts shows no word that clearly means Algarve (the Arabic El-Gharb). Adler's own reading gives the word *Al-Ervah* (which means naked), with other variants listed in his footnotes. When Benjamin is describing Alexandria he lists among the traders the Spaniards, Catalans, Flemish, French, Aragonese, and Navarrese, but not the Portuguese. He states that the Moslems from Andalusia, Algarve (?), Africa, and Arabia were in Alexandria. Spain but not Portugal is mentioned in con-

nection with Constantinople. He describes Thessalonica but does not mention merchants. Nor does he mention the Portuguese in connection with Marseilles. (I am endebted to my colleagues Professors Oscar Janowsky and Howard Adelson, and to Miss Stein of the Jewish Theological Seminary of New York City for aid in examining printed works and manuscripts of Rabbi Benjamin's *Itinerary*.)

4 Finot, *Flandre-Gênes*, pp. 6-9. As noted above in note 17, chapter II, Doehaerd takes the view that there was no trade by crusaders.

5 O. L. Godin, *Princes et princesses de la famille royale de Portugal ayant par leurs alliances régné sur la Flandre: rapports entre la Flandre et le Portugal de 1094 à 1682* (Lisbon, 1892); Almeida, *História Portugal*, I, 168-169, 187-188; *Quadro elementar*, I, 98-99, III, 4, XIV, 2 (gives date incorrectly as 1147); Vandenbussche, *Flandre-Portugal*, pp. 23-27; Veiga Simões, *Flandre-Portugal*, pp. 14-15; Saavedra Machado, in *Biblos*, X, 580-583, XII, 228. Teresa was also known as Mafalda and Mahout.

6 Saavedra Machado, in *Biblos*, X, 583-590, XI, 172-186, 372-388; Michel, *Portugais-Français; Quadro elementar*, III, 4, XIV, 2-3; Gama Barros, *Administração pública*, IX, 314-315; Vandenbussche, *Flandre-Portugal*, pp. 28-29, relying mainly on Flemish sources. See also *Narratio de itinere navali*, ed. Charles Wendell David, *Proceedings of the American Philosophical Society*, vol. 81, no. 5 (December 1939). For the Portuguese view of the Algarve campaigns of 1189 see Frei António Brandão, *Monarchia lusitana*, part IV, bk. 12. There is a new edition edited by A. de Magalhães Basto as *Crónica de D. Sancho I e D. Afonso II* (Oporto, 1945), chs. 7-9. See also Rui de Pina, *Crónica de El-Rei D. Sancho I* (Lisbon, 1906), and other editions.

7 Montalvor, *Régimen republicano*, I, 58; *Quadro elementar*, III, 5, citing the *Narratio de itinere navali* as first edited by Costanzo Gazzera in *Memorie della Reale Academia delle Scienze di Torino, Scienze Morali, Storiche e Filologiche* (2nd series, II, 1840), pp. 177-207. This edition was used by many writers prior to David's edition (and by some since) to justify the statements that merchants from Portugal were seen in Montpellier and Marseilles at the end of the twelfth century. Such an interpretation is possible but doubtful. The Latin text reads: "Et notandum quod postea Massilie et in Montepessulano vidimus mercatores qui in civitatibus Sarracenorum erant cum transsivimus; et nos viderunt et dixerunt quod omnes Sarraceni ita pavefacti erant de transsitu nostro quod nullam civitatem defendissent si eam adiissemus, sed tantum ad fugam preparabant." Translation: "It is to be noted that later, in Marseilles and Montpellier, we saw merchants who were in Saracen towns when we passed through them; and they saw us and told us that all the Saracens were so frightened at our passage that they defended no city if we drew near it, but just prepared to flee."

Among the many authors who have relied on this manuscript are the Baron de Reiffenberg, *Coup d'oeil sur les relations qui ont existé jadis entre la Belgique et le Portugal, Mémoire de l'Académie des Sciences de Bruxelles* (1841); Thieury, *Portugal-Normandie*, pp. 8-10; Magalhães Godinho, *Grandes découvertes,* pp. 27-29; and Almeida, *História Portugal,* I, 457, citing *Quadro elementar,* III, xix, 5 to justify the statement: "Em 1189 já eram freqüentes as relações comerciais de Portugal com Montpelier e Marselha." The historians of these two cities do not bear this out. Although A. Boudin, *Histoire de Marseilles* (Marseilles, 1852), p. 149, says that in the twelfth century Christians and Moslem merchants from Algarve were trading in Marseilles where they met merchants from all parts of the Mediterranean, he gives no citation and his book contains no footnotes. Nor does he equate Algarve with Portugal. Raoul Busquet, *Histoire de Marseilles* (Paris, 1945), says nothing of Portugal. Régine Pernoud, co-author with Raoul Busquet of *Histoire du commerce de Marseilles* (Paris, 1949), relies very largely on L. Blancard, *Documents inédits sur le commerce de Marseilles au Moyen Âge* (2 vols., Marseilles, 1884-1885), says nothing of the Portuguese, though many places in North Africa are mentioned. Augustin Fabre, *Histoire de Marseilles* (2 vols., Paris-Marseilles, 1829), is silent on the Portuguese.

The situation with reference to Montpellier is the same. A. Germain, *Histoire du commerce de Montpellier* (2 vols., Montpellier, 1861), I, 4, quotes Benjamin de Tudela, but does not mention the Portuguese. We may conclude that while it was feasible for merchants from Portugal to reach Montpellier and Marseilles in the twelfth century, no conclusive contemporary evidence shows that they did.

8 Herculano, *História Portugal,* III, 157-212; Almeida, *História Portugal,* I, 176-177, with notes by David Lopes to correct Herculano; Saavedra Machado, in *Biblos, Expedições normandas,* pp. 22 ff.; Michel, *Portugais-Français,* pp. 3-4, with notes.

9 *Quadro elementar,* I, 58, III, 7-9; Almeida, *História Portugal,* I, 178-179. Montalvor, *Régimen republicano,* cites *P.M.H., Scriptores,* I, 100, to show export of salt by the Cistercians, but does not indicate clearly that it was sent abroad. See on this a recent work by Virginia Rau, *A exploração e o comercio do sal de Setúbal* (Lisbon, 1951).

CHAPTER FOUR

1 *Quadro elementar,* III, 5-8, XIV, 4-6. Santarém in his introduction to volume XIV, pp. ix-x, has a misprint which gives the date as 1190 instead of 1199 as in the document. The basic published work for the European treaties of this epoch is Thomas Rymer, *Foedera, conventiones, litterae et cuiuscumque generis acta publica inter Reges Angliae, et alios quosvis . . . ab anno 1101 . . .* (various editions, 10 vols., The Hague, 1739 and later), I, 113, II, 609. Hereafter cited as Rymer, *Foedera.* Also Braamcamp Freire, *Feitoria,* in *A.H.P.,* VI, 323; Vandenbussche, *Flandre-Portugal,* 47-48, 161; Saavedra Machado, in *Biblos,* XII, 228-229; V. M. Shillington and A. B. Wallis Chapman, *The Commercial Relations of England and Portugal* (London, 1907), pp. 3-4, hereafter cited as Shillington, *England-Portugal.* Herculano, *História Portugal,* III, 212 ff.

2 The act of Philip II of France reads: "omnia averia que transeunt de Flandria sive in Franciam, sive in Burgumdium, sive ultra montes, sive

Provinciam, debent pedagiam apud Bapalmes, etc." According to Cantineau, *Flandre-Portugal*, the phrase *ultra montes* was translated *d'outre les montes d'Espagne* in the thirteenth century. He cites another document in Flemish which states that "Limoges and Pamplona are on the same route to Spain and Santiago in Galicia," and he says that the merchants went on to Saragossa, Toledo, other towns in Spain, and to Lisbon. He thinks the evidence justifies the belief that trade between Flanders and Portugal began with the pilgrimages to Santiago and was stimulated by the crusaders. Furthermore, he says that Spanish and Portuguese merchants brought their own products to Flanders, as witnessed by the entries in the customs records of Bapaume in 1202. He cites Meyer, Reiffenberg, Vandenbussche, and Kervyn de Lettenhove, all mentioned above, and archives in Lille, Bruges, and Ghent. Nevertheless, from the Latin text above, Italy could as well have been *ultra montes* as Spain and Portugal. Veiga Simões, *Flandre-Portugal*, uses a manuscript published by Legrand d'Aussey, *Fabliaux*, volume IV, to substantiate the early Flemish-Portuguese trade.

3 Marcelo Caetano, "A administração municipal de Lisboa durante a primeira dinastia," in *Revista da Faculdade de Direito da Universidade de Lisboa,* VII (1950), 5-112, VIII (1951), 149-212.

4 Shillington, *England-Portugal,* pp. 24-26.

5 Gama Barros, *Administração pública,* IX, 319; *Quadro elementar,* I, 20; João Martins da Silva Marques, *Descobrimentos portugueses* (one volume and *suplemento,* Lisbon, 1944), I, p. 2, document 4. This work is to be preferred over the *Quadro elementar* when both carry the same document. Hereafter cited as Silva Marques, *Descobrimentos.*

6 Vandenbussche, *Flandre-Portugal,* pp. 30-38; *Quadro elementar,* III, 9-10, XIV, 6; Michel, *Portugais-Français,* pp. 6 ff.; Saavedra Machado, in *Biblos,* XII, 436-454. The Biblioteca da Ajuda in Lisbon contains a manuscript entitled: "Faits de Baudouin Comte de Flandres et de Ferrant, fis de Sance, Roy de Portugal, et successeur de Baudouin, dan la fin du siècle XII," but its accuracy is questionable, or would at least require an amount of verification not useful to this study.

7 Saavedra Machado, *Expedições normandas,* p. 24, and in *Biblos,* XIII, 168-183, gives an extensive bibliography for this period. Other material in Almeida, *História Portugal,* I, 187-201; *Quadro elementar,* III, 10, XIV, 6; Rui de Pina, *Crónica de El-Rei D. Afonso II* (Lisbon, 1906) and other editions; Frei António Brandão, *Monarchia lusitana,* part IV, bk. 13, recently reprinted as cited in chapter III, note 6 above.

8 R. Francisque-Michel, *Histoire du commerce et de la navigation à Bordeaux* (2 vols., Bordeaux, 1867-1870), II, 154-155; Michel, *Portugais-Français,* pp. 101-102, 167-168; Shillington, *England-Portugal,* pp. 26-28; *Quadro elementar,* XIV, 7; Gama Barros, *Administração pública,* IX, 313-319. The statement that Genoese ships were in the Atlantic trade as early as 1242 rests on Michel, but is uncertain. He could have accurately mentioned Portuguese ships in French waters in this period.

9 Almeida, *História Portugal,* I, 209-213, 216-219, 235-236; *Quadro elementar,* III, 11-12; Frei António Brandão, *Monarchia lusitana,* part IV, bks. 14 and 15, recently edited by A. de Magalhães Basto, *Crónica de D. Sancho II e D. Afonso III* (Oporto, 1946); Rui de Pina, *Crónica de El-Rei D. Afonso III* (Lisbon, 1907) and other editions.

10 Almeida, *História Portugal,* I, 221-223; Gama Barros, *Administração pública,* IX, 315-316, X, 221-280; Braamcamp Freire, *Feitoria,* pp. 42-43; Silva Marques, *Descobrimentos,* I, p. 6, doc. 9; Montalvor, *Régimen republicano,* I, 58-59; Antonio Ballesteros Beretta, *Sevilla en el siglo XIII,* pp. 25-49; F. Salles Lencastre, *Estudo sobre as portagens e as alfândegas em Portugal* (Lisbon, 1891), pp. 1-2, 12-13; Eduardo Freire de Oliveira, *Elementos para a história do municipio de Lisboa* (19 vols., Lisbon, 1882-1911), with numerous documents on the period in volume I; *Quadro elementar,* III, 12-13, XIV, 7, which gives the date in error as 1252, which Almeida also does in a number of places.

11 Silva Marques, *Descobrimentos,* I, p. 7, doc. 10; *Quadro elementar,* III, 13, which erroneously states that one-third of French shipping must discharge in Gaia, whereas it was half in Gaia and half in Oporto, but he gives the correct division in I, 20. Almeida and Gama Barros cited in note 10 are both useful.

12 Silva Marques, *Descobrimentos,* I, *suplemento,* p. 9, doc. 4, says this date, given in Herculano, *História Portugal,* V, 306, is almost certainly wrong.

13 The materials used from here to the end of the chapter are covered in Gama Barros, *Administração pública,* IX, 315 ff.; Silva Marques, *Descobrimentos,* I, pp. 8-17, docs. 12-21; Shillington, *England-Portugal,* pp. 30 ff.; Pedro de Azevedo, "O porto franco de Caminha no século XIV," in *Revista de História,* I (1912), 105, with documents; Vandenbussche, *Flandre-Portugal,* pp. 45-48.

CHAPTER FIVE

1 Almeida, *História Portugal,* I, 235-257, 321-325; Rau, *Feiras medievais,* pp. 23-25; Rui de Pina, *Crónica de D. Dinis* (Oporto, 1945) and other editions.

2 Pirenne, *Histoire Belgique,* I, 245-250, who cites Warnkoenig, *Flandre,* II, 512-516, and K. Höhlbaum, *Hansisches urkundenbuch,* I, 150.

3 Gama Barros, *Administração pública,* X, 207-220; Vandenbussche, *Flandre-Portugal,* pp. 49, 169-170; Cantineau, *Flandre-Portugal,* pp. 15-27; Bruyssel, *Commerce belgique,* I, 233-234; Braamcamp Freire, *Feitoria,* pp. 36, 48 *et seq., passim.*

4 Montalvor, *Régimen republicano,* I, 49; Silva Marques, *Descobrimentos,* I, pp. 13-17, docs. 19-21; Alberto Iria, *Descobrimentos portugueses: O Algarve e os descobrimentos* (Lisbon, 1956), vol. II, tome L, pp. 266 ff., has an abundance of information on the commerce of Algarve in this and later periods. Iria's work is called the second part of the *Descobrimentos* of which Silva Marques is editor, and is consequently called volume II, divided into two tomes. Hereafter cited as Iria, *Descobrimentos.*

5 Gama Barros, *Administração pública*, IX, 328, X, 327; *Quadro elementar,* I, 20, III, 13-16, relying on *Recueil des ordonnances des rois de France,* II, 157. See also Rymer, *Foedera,* 3rd ed., II, 509, 627, 631, 667, 691; Shillington, *England-Portugal,* pp. 4-5, 26-35, using the Patent Rolls as a source; Thomas Carte, *Catalogue des rolles gascons, normans, et françois* (2 vols., London, 1743), which contains treaties, *salvoconductos,* etc., dating from the end of the thirteenth century; Michel, *Commerce de Bordeaux,* II, 154, n. 5, and *Portugais-Français,* pp. 168-169, who uses Rymer, *Foedera,* the *Rolles gascons,* and numerous secondary works; Silva Marques, *Descobrimentos,* I, *sup.,* pp. 17-19, docs. 12-14; Veiga Simões, *Flandre-Portugal,* with a good discussion of the nature of medieval Portuguese commerce. For French trade, see an excellent recent work by Michel Mollat, *Le commerce maritime normand à la fin du Moyen Âge* (Paris, 1952), pp. 3-63, with an excellent bibliography.

6 The *pustura* is one of the famous documents in Portuguese history and has been published a number of times. See Silva Marques, *Descobrimentos,* I, pp. 21-22, doc. 29, where other places of publication are listed. All historians covering the period rely on it. Discussions may be found in Gama Barros, *Administração pública,* IX, 357 ff.; Shillington, *England-Portugal,* 31 ff., and Jaime Cortesão in Montalvor, *Régimen republicano,* I, 61 ff. Cortesão takes the reasonable view that *além mar* meant North Africa, as well as the more questionable position that it also meant the Levant. Certainly the Portuguese *could* have traded in the Levant, but aside from the evidence of Timarion there is not much documentary evidence. For the values of Portuguese coins see Augusto Carlos Teixeira de Aragão, *Descripção geral e histórica das moedas . . . de Portugal* (3 vols., Lisbon, 1874-1880), I, 169 *et seq., passim.*

7 Gama Barros, *Administração pública,* IX, 318, n. 5, citing Charles Jourdain, *Excursion historique et philosophiques à travers le Moyen Âge, Mémoire sur les commencements de la marine militaire sous Philip le Bel, Mémoire de l'Académie des Inscriptions et Belles Lettres,* XX (1888), 402; and Michel, *Portugais-Français,* p. 169, who cites the same work by Jourdain.

8 Magalhães ⁀Godinho, *Grandes découvertes,* pp. 23-24; *Documentos do Arquivo Histórico da Câmara Municipal de Lisboa, Livro de Reis* (Lisbon, 1957), I, 31-32; Silva Marques, *Descobrimentos,* I, *sup.,* pp. 21-25, doc. 15; *Quadro elementar,* I, 120-127.

9 Braamcamp Freire, *Feitoria,* p. 48; *Quadro elementar,* I, 67, XIV, 17-18; Shillington, *England-Portugal,* pp. 35-47; Gama Barros, *Administração pública,* IX, 360-361, X, 207; Vandenbussche, *Flandre-Portugal,* pp. 193-201.

10 Lencastre, *Portagens,* pp. 15-16; *Quadro elementar,* XIV, 18-22; Silva Marques, *Descobrimentos,* I, *sup.,* p. 26, doc. 16.

11 Gama Barros, *Administração pública,* X, 281-291; Charles Verlinden, *Deux aspects de l'expansion commerciale du Portugal au Moyen Âge,* offprint from *Revista Portuguesa de História,* IV (1947), who gives a new reading of the 1310 grant of privilege made to the Portuguese by Philip IV of France.

12 Veiga Simões, *Flandre-Portugal,* pp. 17-30; Émile Varenbergh, *Les relations des Pays-Bas avec le Portugal et l'Espagne d'après un écrivain du XVIIe siècle,* in *Annales de l'Academie Royale d'Archeólogie de Belgique,* XXV (1869), 2nd series, V, 10 ff., based on a manuscript of François le Blanc (d. 1698) in the Ghent archives.

CHAPTER SIX

1 Michele Amari, *Nuovi ricordi arabici su la storia di Genova,* in *Atti della Società Ligure di Storia Patria,* V (Genova, 1858-1942), 591-617; Canale, *Genova,* I, 229 ff., 304 ff., 332 ff. For Italian contacts in the East, see Robert S. Lopez, "European Merchants in the Medieval Indies: the Evidence of the Commercial Documents," in *The Journal of Economic History,* III (1943), 164-184.

2 E. H. Byrne, *Genoese Shipping in the Twelfth and Thirteenth Century* (Cambridge, Mass., 1930), pp. 28-49; Isidore François Hye Hoys, *Fondation pieuses et charitables des marchands flamands en Espagne* (Brussels, 1882), pp. 28-29, reprinted from *Précis Historique,* XXXI, or 2nd series, XI (1882), 297-326, 376-401, 489-513, 557-578; Roberto S. Lopez, *L'attività economica a Genova nel marzo 1253,* in *Atti della Società Ligure di Storia Patria,* LXIV (Genova, 1935), 177 and 215; and also Roberto S. Lopez, "Majorcans and Genoese on the North Sea Route in the Thirteenth Century," in *Revue Belge de Philologie et Histoire,* XXIX (1951), no. 4; Prospero Peragallo, *Cenni intorno alla colonia italiana in Portogallo nei secoli XIV, XV, XVI* (2nd ed., Genova, 1907), pp. 50-52, 168-179 *et seq., passim;* A. A. Ruddock, *Italian Merchants and Shipping in Southampton, 1270-1700* (Southampton, 1951), pp. 14 ff. Ruddock cites among others Canale and Byrne. Also see Doehaerd, *Gênes-Belgique,* II, 221 ff.; Lopez, *Genova Marinara,* pp. 48-49.

3 Po in Federzoni, *Italia-Portogallo,* pp. 266 ff.; Roberto S. Lopez, *Storia delle colonie genovese nel Mediterraneo* (Bologna, 1938), pp. 312-316, 458-463; Gama Barros, *Administração pública,* X, 171-196; Michel, *Commerce de Bordeaux,* I, 159 ff.; Francis M. Rogers, *The Vivaldi Expedition,* offprint from 73rd *Annual Report of the Dante Society* (n.d.); A. Cauchie and L. van der Essen, *Les sources de l'histoire nationale conservés à l'etranter dans les archives privées,* in *Bulletin, Commission d'Histoire, Académie Royale Belgique,* LXXVIII (1909), 46-102. The authors rely on Finot, cited in chapter II, note 6, above.

4 Finot, *Flandre-Gênes,* pp. 20-31; Ruddock, *Italian Merchants,* pp. 20 ff.; Doehaerd, *Gênes Belgique,* II, 224-236; A. Pinchart, *Du commerce des Belges avec les Vénetiens du XIIe au XVIe siècles,* in *Messager des Sciences et des Arts* (Ghent, 1851), pp. 9-25; Bruyssel, *Commerce belgique,* I, 307 ff.

5 Information concerning the Venetians in Portugal prior to 1392 has been strangely lacking, considering their importance and the documentation on the Florentines, Genoese, and other foreigners. In 1309, as noted, what could have been an order of expulsion was issued. See Silva Marques, *Descobrimentos,* I, *sup.,* p. 385, doc. 314, and Conde de Tovar, *Portugal e Veneza na Idade-Média até 1495* (Coimbra, 1933), pp. 17-24, 65-67. The long

gap from 1309 to 1392 suggested that the order of 1309 might have been effective in keeping the Venetians out. However, Iria in *Descobrimentos,* vol. II, tome I, 253, 292-294, 356, 383, 398, shows the presence of Venetians in Portugal after 1309. Two recently discovered documents, found in the Archivio di Stato, Venice, show definitely that the Venetians were in Portugal in 1374 and 1375. The Conde de Tovar did not discover these when he was preparing his study. One is a power plenipotentiary to a representative of the Venetian Senate to protest an order of reprisal directed against the Venetians by King Fernando. It is in the *Sindicati,* dated March 21, 1374. The other is Fernando's reply, July 13, 1375, in *Commemoriali,* VII, number 831. This document is listed by António Ferrão in "Notícia de algumas espécies portuguesas, ou relativas ao nosso país, existentes em bibliotecas e arquivos estranjeiros," in *Anais das Bibliotecas e Arquivos,* XXI (Lisbon, 1951), 80. Fernando excuses himself, denies that he intended reprisals, and refers to the "ancient friendship" of the two peoples in such terms as to indicate regular and friendly relations. Furthermore, he says that a search had failed to reveal any act against the Venetians during the time of his predecessors. Whatever the explanation for the scarcity of documents relating to the Venetians, they apparently carried on commerce with Portugal during the fourteenth century.

6 The Italian spelling was sometimes Pessagno and at other times Pezagno. See José Benedito de Almeida Pessanha, *Os Almirantes Pessanhas e sua descendência* (Oporto, 1923); and Luigi Tomasso Belgrano, *Documenti e genealogia dei Pessagno, genovesi, ammiragli del Portogallo,* in *Atti della Società Ligure di Storia Patria,* XV (1882), 241-316.

7 Silva Marques, *Descobrimentos,* I, pp. 27-32, docs. 37-40; Almeida, *História Portugal,* I, 251, with references covering the period; Peragallo, *Colonia italiana,* pp. 6-9; Gama Barros, *Administração pública,* IX, 319 ff.; Po in Federzoni, *Italia-Portogallo,* p. 284 *et seq., passim.*

8 Po in Federzoni, *Italia-Portogallo,* pp. 261-262, an Italian author, takes a position which credits the Italians with practically all discoveries. Magalhães Godinho, in *Grandes découvertes,* pp. 25 ff., a Portuguese, is positive that the documents show that Peçanha was called to Lisbon solely to help create a war fleet of *galés.* Both men use essentially the same documents. The difference is consequently the opposition of two national prides. Another point made by Magalhães Godinho is that the Atlantic required a type of vessel different from the Mediterranean galley, the Atlantic being so much rougher. While the Atlantic no doubt offers navigational problems more difficult than the Mediterranean where a "lost" ship can make a landfall more easily, it may be noted that modern ships sometimes go down in Mediterranean storms.

The problem of food and water was perhaps the most important difference between sailing the Mediterranean and the Atlantic. And it is in this field that type of ships built in Portugal and Spain were superior, though there is no doubt that Italians helped here also. Two things would seem to have contributed most to the ability to make long voyages: the caravel was a superior sailing vessel, and with it there was no need to feed the large number of rowers used to propel the galley. Morison estimates that the number of men in the crew of a caravel was probably about one-tenth those needed in a galley. Samuel Eliot Morison, *Admiral of the Ocean Sea* (2 vols., Boston, 1942), I, xxi-xxii.

9 Peragallo, *Italia-Portogallo*, pp. 69, 77 ff., 139 ff.; José Benedito de Almeida Pessanha, *Noticia histórica dos Almirantes Pessanhas* (Lisbon, 1900), and *Os Almirantes Pessanhas*, cited in note 6 above. On the use made of the Peçanhas as diplomats by both England and Portugal, see Shillington, *England-Portugal*, pp. 6 ff.; and Santarém in *Quadro elementar*, XIV, 24-28.

10 Silva Marques, *Descobrimentos*, I, pp. 33, 42, 44, docs. 41, 48, 50, and *sup.*, pp. 27-28, docs. 17, 18; Montalvor, *Régimen republicano*, I, 71; *Quadro elementar*, XIV, 23-24, and I, 148; Thieury, *Portugal-Normandie*, pp. 10-12; Braamcamp Freire, *Feitoria*, pp. 48-49.

11 Silva Marques, *Descobrimentos*, I, p. 53, doc. 57, and *sup.*, pp. 29-30, doc. 20; Gama Barros, *Administração pública*, X, 199-201. The charters of privilege granted to foreign traders are one of the chief sources for the economic history of this period. See a useful publication by H. V. Livermore, "The Privileges of an Englishman in the Kingdoms and Dominions of Portugal," *Atlante*, II (1954), no. 2. The originals of many such charters, if they still exist, are found in the Arquivo Nacional da Torre do Tombo, Lisbon. Many copies were made, however, for those receiving the privileges, for diplomats, and others, and these are found in many libraries in Portugal and other countries. The British Museum has such copies in the Lansdowne Collection, number 190, Additional Manuscript number 27,344, the Harley Collection, numbers 3554, 3555 (folio 255 ff.), and the Egerton Collection, number 527. The University of Coimbra Library has copies in manuscripts 324, 699, 784, 1254, 2569, and 2574.

12 *Quadro elementar*, I, 58, III, 18-21; Silva Marques, *Descobrimentos*, I, pp. 75-76, docs. 66-68; Thieury, *Portugal-Normandie*, pp. 14-27, 71-90; Shillington, *England-Portugal*, p. 39.

13 Almeida, *História Portugal*, I, 268-271; Silva Marques, *Descobrimentos*, I, pp. 77-90, docs. 69-75; Rogers, *Vivaldi Expedition*, cited in note 3 above; *Quadro elementar*, I, 186-188; Peragallo, *Colonia italiana*, pp. 9 ff.; Charles de la Roncière, *La découverte de l'Afrique au Moyen Âge* (3 vols., Cairo, 1924-1927), II, 3 ff.; Magalhães Godinho, *Grandes découvertes*, pp. 17 ff., who presents the view that there were a number of Portuguese voyages; Po, in *Mundo português*, III, 579 ff., who stresses the Italian character of the early voyages to the Canaries; and Almeida, *História Portugal*, III, 759-789, who publishes documents purporting to show other Portuguese discoveries later in the fourteenth century. He also shows that his documents have not been accepted as unquestionably authentic. See below, ch. VII, n. 4.

The whole question of what to accept as evidence for the early Atlantic voyages is still open. Some writers have used an account attributed to an anonymous Franciscan sometime presumably close to 1350. This work, given the title of *Libro del Conoscimiento*, relates a journey, real or imaginary, of the friar from Spain to extensive regions of Europe, Asia, and Africa.

It was undoubtedly written after considerable exploration had been done along the African coast. But if the Franciscan traveled at all, he was a very poor observer and left us an incredibly deficient account. Florentino Pérez Embid, in *Los descubrimientos en el Atlántico y la rivalidad castellano-portuguesa hasta el tratado de Tordesillas* (Sevilla, 1948), pp. 54-58, shows the doubts that have been expressed about this work. Although accepted as authentic by Jaime Cortesão in *Historia Portugal Monumental,* ed. Damião Peres, III, 347, Peres himself in his *Descobrimentos portugueses,* pp. 20-21, classifies it as a *romance geográfico* of the same stamp as Sir John Mandeville's *Travels.* The *Libro,* for example, says that African ants were as large as European cats! Should we understand from this that African ants were really so large or that European cats were small?

Until there is more genuine documentation, we cannot draw overoptimistic conclusions about explorations of the Atlantic coastline of Africa, by Portuguese or others, prior to Prince Henry's discoveries.

14 Shillington, *England-Portugal,* pp. 7 ff., 41 ff., 66 ff.; *Quadro elementar,* I, 59, III, 21, XIV, 28-46; Silva Marques, *Descobrimentos,* I, pp. 90-97, docs. 76, 79, 80, and *sup.,* pp. 33-34, doc. 23.

15 On national development see Magalhães Godinho, *Grandes découvertes,* pp. 20 ff.; and Jaime Cortesão in Montalvor, *Régimen republicano,* I, 70-71, to which can be added his "Teoria geral dos descobrimentos portugueses," in *Mundo português,* III, 11-46.

CHAPTER SEVEN

1 Silva Marques, *Descobrimentos,* I, pp. 105-116, docs. 83-89, 95, 101; Fernão Lopes, *Chrónica de El-Rei D. Pedro I* (Lisbon, 1895), and *Chrónica de El-Rei D. Fernando* (Lisbon, 1895-1896), or other editions of both chronicles; Montalvor, *Régimen republicano,* I, 60 ff.; *Documentos do Arquivo de Lisboa: Livro de Reis,* I, 37-38, 130-131.

2 Silva Marques, *Descobrimentos,* I, pp. 116-121, docs. 102, 104, 106; *Quadro elementar,* I, 59, 67, III, 21-25, XIV, 47; Gama Barros, *Administração pública,* IX, 343-344; Shillington, *England-Portugal,* pp. 49 ff., who confuses the *escorcins* (i.e., Cahorsins) with Scots, mistakenly saying that the Scots were among those who received privileges in Portugal; Thieury, *Portugal-Normandie,* pp. 13-14, 28.

3 Almeida, *História Portugal,* I, 286-290; Silva Marques, *Descobrimentos,* I, pp. 121-145, docs. 107-110, 114, 116, 123, 125, 126, 129, and *sup.,* pp. 47-48, doc. 37; *Quadro elementar,* I, 21, 68, 215-216, 230, III, 29, XIV, 47-48; Shillington, *England-Portugal,* pp. 48-52; Peragallo, *Colonia italiana,* pp. 92, 158-159.

4 Attention was called in chapter VI, note 13, to the uncertainties concerning the discoveries of the Canary Islands and other Atlantic areas in the fourteenth century. The documents published by Almeida, *História Portugal,* III, 759 ff., add to the confusion. By a charter dated June 29, 1370, Fernando granted to Lançarote da Franca two unpopulated islands called

Nossa Senhora a Franca and Gomeira, supposedly in the region of Cape Nun (Cabo Não) on the African coast. He is given the title of Admiral and spoken of as the discoverer and conqueror *(as yllas que trobou e nos gaañou)* and invested with the government. In July 1376 he was given other properties in Portugal in compensation for the expenses he incurred when attempting to occupy the islands in the face of Castilian and native *(sic)* resistance. The authenticity of the documents was questioned by Afonso de Dornelas in a critique also published by Almeida. Jaime Cortesão, who presented the documents before the Academia das Ciências de Lisboa, upheld them and concluded that the explorations had been continuous since 1336, or 1341, whichever date is accepted for the voyages to the Canaries spoken of above in chapter VI. A few questions raised are: Was Lançarote da Franca the same as Lançarote Peçanha the admiral? If he "found and won" the islands for King Fernando, the discovery date would have to be after 1367 when Fernando came to the throne, in which case, are they part of the Canaries, as their names indicate? If so, what becomes of the earlier Portuguese voyage or voyages, and of the Italian settlement, now usually placed at least as early as 1312? There are no documented answers to these questions. As far as research has now gone, we remain largely in doubt. So many have suggested solutions to the problems that one more possible solution may not be out of order. One of the Canaries is named Lançarote after its supposed discoverer, an Italian. The time, 1312, is not far removed from that when Peçanha and his twenty captains came to serve Dinís in 1317. Could the Lançarote of the island have a link with one of the captains in such a way as to justify Fernando's grant to Lança-rote da Franca? There is no evidence of this; it is put forward merely as a line of research.

Damião Peres in his *História dos descobrimentos portugueses* (Oporto, 1943), pp. 9-21, does not mention the documents published by Almeida. Silva Marques, *Descobrimentos,* I, pp. 126-127, 155, 186, docs. 115, 137, 162, reproduces them with a promise to comment in the still unpublished introduction to his collection. A bit more documentation and a bit less nationalism might help clarify the disputed points. Meanwhile, by comparing Peres with Pérez Embid, *Los descubrimientos en el Atlántico,* pp. 69-110, a fairly well-balanced view can be achieved.

5 P. E. Russell, *The English Intervention in Spain and Portugal in the Time of Edward III and Richard II* (Oxford, The Clarendon Press, 1955), chs. 7, 9, 14-20; *Quadro elementar,* III, 30, XIV, 49-59; Shillington, *England-Portugal,* pp. 8-10; Thieury, *Portugal-Normandie,* p. 12; Silva Marques, *Descobrimentos,* I, pp. 138-140, docs. 120-122; Caetano, "Administração Lisboa," in *Revista Direito,* VII, 50; Almeida, *História Portugal,* I, 289-292.

6 Gama Barros, *Administração pública,* IX, 96, 345-346, 361; Silva Marques, *Descobrimentos,* I, p. 145, doc. 128; Almeida, *História Portugal,* I, 292-293; Fernão Lopes, *Crónica de Dom Fernando,* preliminary chapter; Montalvor, *Régimen republicano,* I, 64, 81-82.

7 Shillington, *England-Portugal,* pp. 50-54; *Quadro elementar,* I, 21, XIV, 59; Gama Barros, *Administração pública,* X, 171-196, 211-212; Lencastre, *Porta-*

gens, pp. 19-22; Silva Marques, *Descobrimentos,* I, pp. 156-157, 168-170, docs.
138, 145, and *sup.,* pp. 51-60, doc. 42; Braamcamp Freire, *Feitoria,* pp. 35-37;
Michel, *Portugais-Français,* p. 171.

8 *Documentos Arquivo Lisboa, Livro de Reis,* I, 346-347; Silva Marques,
Descobrimentos, I, pp. 158-178, docs. 140, 141, 147, 148, 151; Almeida, *His-
tória Portugal,* I, 293-294; Lencastre, *Portagens,* pp. 22 ff.; Gama Barros,
Administração pública, IX, 357 ff.; Azevedo, "Porto franco Caminha," in
Revista de História, I, 105; Fernão Lopes, *Crónica Fernando,* ch. 91.

9 Karl Reatz, *Geschichte des Europäischen Seeversicherungsrechts* (Leipzig,
1870), I, 14, 52 ff., 72, 91.

10 Gama Barros, *Administração pública,* IX, 359; Silva Marques, *Descobrimentos,* I, p. 207, doc. 193.

11 A. Goris, *Études sur les colonies marchandes méridionales, portugais,
espagnoles, italiens, à Anvers de 1488 à 1567* (Louvain, 1925), pp. 178-179.

12 Gama Barros, *Administração pública,* IX, 381-383; Michel, *Portugais-
Français,* pp. 274-277.

13 Almeida, *História Portugal,* I, 296-303; Shillington, *England-Portugal,* pp.
10-12, 50-52; *Quadro elementar,* I, 248, XIV, 59-70.

CHAPTER EIGHT

1 João's succession to the throne is one of the favorite topics of Portuguese
historians. The question is: To what extent was the "new" nobility new —
was it old agrarian or new commercial? Quite obviously new families of
landholders rose to prominence, but also quite obviously they were connected with Portugal's commercial interests, and the new dynasty was to
look after the interests of both aspects of the economy. For a discussion of
these points with an accompanying bibliography, see Almeida, *História
Portugal,* I, 304-316; and Montalvor, *Régimen republicano,* I, 99 ff. An
excellent recent discussion is by Marcello Caetano, "As cortes de 1385," in
Revista Portuguesa de História, V (1951), 5-85. The contemporary and
official chronicle is Fernão Lopes, *Crónica de El-Rei d. João I,* of which
there are various editions.

Luis Suárez Fernández points out that the defeat of Castile on land in
1385 also broke her naval power and thus gave Portugal a lead in Atlantic
exploration. The merchants of Lisbon and Oporto, foreseeing the consequences adverse to their own interests if Portugal should become subject to
Castile, combined to break the naval blockade of Lisbon. Castile, still
occupied with the war against Portugal and involved with internal troubles
during the reign of Juan II and later, could not match Portugal's commercial and maritime vigor. See Luis Suárez Fernández, "El Atlántico y el
Mediterráneo en los objetivos políticos de la casa de Trastamara," in *Revista
Portuguesa de Historia,* V (1951), 287-307.

2 Silva Marques, *Descobrimentos,* I, pp. 185 ff., docs. 160, 173, 192, and *sup.,*
pp. 63-68, docs. 46-48; P. E. Russell, "Galés portuguesas ao serviço de

Ricardo II de Inglaterra (1385-1389)," in *Revista da Faculdade de Letras,* 2nd series, XVIII (1953); *Quadro elementar,* III, 36, XIV, 70-106; Russell, *English Intervention in Spain and Portugal,* pp. 400-448; Freire de Oliveira, *Elementos história Lisboa,* I, 255-263.

3 Charles Verlinden, "Le problème de l'expansion commerciale portugaise au Moyen Âge," in *Biblos,* XXIII (1947), 452-467, and Verlinden, cited in chapter V, note 11 above; Varenbergh, *Pays-Bas-Portugal,* pp. 14 ff.; Braam-camp Freire, *Feitoria,* pp. 48-50; Vandenbussche, *Flandre-Portugal,* pp. 50-51; Silva Marques, *Descobrimentos,* I, *sup.,* pp. 66-67, doc. 47; *Quadro elementar,* I, 68, 82, XIV, 100.

4 Silva Marques, *Descobrimentos,* I, pp. 194-212, 603-609, docs. 176-200, and *sup.,* pp. 71-72, doc. 53; *Quadro elementar,* I, 21, 22, 59, 66, III, 38, XIV, 115-134; Gama Barros, *Administração pública,* IX, 313-377, X, 171-196; Thieury, *Portugal-Normandie,* pp. 28-29; Michel, *Portugais-Français,* pp. 8-10.

5 Some historians see the pressure for foodstuffs as a prime reason for Portuguese expansion, Magalhães Godinho in *Grandes découvertes,* for example. However, the regions penetrated in Africa were not wheat growing. Shillington, *England-Portugal,* pp. 58-63 gives details of imports from England and other northern regions.

6 Silva Marques, *Descobrimentos,* I, pp. 213, 217-219, 610, docs. 202, 208-210; *Quadro elementar,* I, 22, 23, 68, 69, XIV, 137-151; Jacques Heers, "L'expansion maritime portugaise à la fin du Moyen Âge: la Méditerranée," in *Revista da Faculdade de Letras, Universidade de Lisboa,* 2nd series, XXII (1956), 84-112. emphasizes the Portuguese trade in the Mediterranean in the fifteenth century. He relies mainly on Édouard Baratier and Félix Reynaud, *Histoire du commerce de Marseilles* (Marseilles, 1954), II, 554-558, which does not give enough specific information to bear out Heer's emphasis during the period prior to our termination date, 1415. Later the Portuguese were much more active in Mediterranean trade.

7 Verlinden, in *Biblos,* cited in note 3 above; Lencastre, *Portagens,* pp. 27-34; Vandenbussche, *Flandre-Portugal,* pp. 51-52, 173-187, and in the review *La Flandre,* VIII (1876), 219 ff.; Varenbergh, *Pays-Bas-Portugal,* pp. 12-14; Braamcamp Freire, *Feitoria,* pp. 50-55, 128-133; Silva Marques, *Descobrimentos,* I, pp. 221-231, docs. 215, 216, 222, and *sup.,* pp. 82-88, doc. 62; *Quadro elementar,* I, 60, 82, XIV, 163; Gama Barros, *Administração pública,* X, 208-210.

8 Some readers, seeking to find in Portugal the conventional picture of the other areas of medieval Europe, will want to know something of two subjects not treated here: the role of the Jews and the commercial guilds in Portuguese expansion. The reason for the omission is very simple. There is no documentation that demonstrates any important contribution of either before 1415.

The occupations of the Jews were largely small-scale money-lending and certain trades, such as tailoring, silver and gold smithy, or even astrology.

As in other nations, they were herded into special quarters, required to observe curfew, often robbed, the debts owed to them repudiated, and despised by the Christian population. They enter the pages of history most often when the kings intervened to protect them. They played no important part in wholesale trade or foreign commerce before 1415. The reason is perhaps easy to discover. Portuguese kings and nobles were themselves active in commerce, as has been pointed out. Some Jews could have been their agents, but not the principals. If the Jews played a more important role in foreign commerce after 1415, that is a matter with which this book is not concerned.

Information concerning guilds in Portugal is extremely scarce. That the merchants of Lisbon and Oporto had sufficient cohesion to draw up agreements among themselves, such as the famous *pustura* of 1293, is evident. But aside from this there is not much evidence. As late as the time of Fernando their organization seems to have been rudimentary, certainly nothing to compare with that in other parts of Europe. They spoke as a body in certain meetings of the *Côrtes*, but one of their chief complaints shows their weakness: they complained that king, queen, nobles, bishops, and abbots carried on commerce. From this we may judge that they exercised no monopoly and no great power. Furthermore, a large part of the shipping of Portugal was done by the colonies of foreigners. Their presence in Portugal to a certain extent would have lessened the development of merchant guilds. What little is known about Portuguese organization at home and in foreign ports was mentioned in connection with the *feitoria*.

One type of organization that was to influence shipping, fishing, and eventually exploration to some extent was the *companha* — the agreement between ship captain and crew about the division of the profits of a trip. Such agreements were renegotiated for each trip, and should not be confused with a *companhia*, or joint stock company, for which there is little valid evidence in the fifteenth century. On Jews, guilds, and *companhas*, see Almeida, *História Portugal*, II, 162 ff., 203 ff., III, 194-212; *História Portugal Monumental*, II, 431-444, 532 ff.; Virginia Rau and Bailey W. Diffie, "Alleged Fifteenth-Century Portuguese Joint-Stock Companies and the Articles of Dr. Fitzler," in *The Bulletin of the Institute of Historical Research*, XXVI (London University, 1953), 181-199.

CHAPTER NINE

1 The basic accounts for the period are Gomes Eannes de Zurara (Azurara), *Crónica da tomada de Ceuta por El-Rei D. João I* (Coimbra, 1915); and Mattheus de Pisano, *Livro da guerra de Ceuta escrito . . . em 1460* (Lisbon, 1915), the latter largely taken from the former. Azurara wrote about 1450. Also of importance for the period are the *Crónicas* of Fernão Lopes covering the reigns of Pedro I (1357-1367), Fernando (1367-1383), and João I (1385-1433). There are various editions of these. Modern scholars have written extensively with but little more evidence than given in the contemporary accounts listed above, but with widely divergent viewpoints. Almeida, *História Portugal,* II, 7-25, covers the reign of João I and gives

extensive references. J. Lúcio de Azevedo, *Épocas de Portugal económico* (2nd ed., Lisbon, 1947), pp. 57-67, is considered a modern classic. For a thorough and rational account see two almost identical works by David Lopes in Peres (ed.), *História Portugal Monumental*, III, 385-406, and in Baião (ed.), *História expansão portuguesa*, I, 131-142.

2 Pérez Embid, *Los descubrimientos y la rivalidad castellana-portuguesa*, pp. 46-48, 69-136, for a Spanish viewpoint; Baião (ed.), *História expansão portuguesa*, I, 269-290; Peres (ed.), *História Portugal Monumental*, III, 333-351; and Peres, *Descobrimentos portugueses*, pp. 5-74, for the Portuguese view.

3 Altamira, *España*, I, 609. The official chronicle of the reign of Enrique III of Castile does not record this, but a seventeenth-century historian, Gil González Dávila, *Historia de la vida y hechos del rey Don Henrique III de Castilla* (Madrid, 1638), p. 148, and Luis del Marmol Carvajal, *Descripción general de Africa* (Granada, 1573), vol. II, part 1, fl. 131 r., both mention it. David Lopes, in Peres, *História Portugal Monumental*, III, 538, note 1, doubts the episode. The descriptions indicate, however, that a destruction had taken place and that the town was later sparsely inhabited. Furthermore, such an act was in keeping with the wars that prevailed between Christians of Spain and the Moslems of North Africa and Spain.

4 The caravel of the discoveries was a development of the fifteenth century and lies beyond the scope of this book. Although a vessel of the same name had existed at least since the mid-thirteenth century, and was probably named after the Moslem *carib,* the ship we are discussing was in effect new. The first recorded voyage of this type of caravel was Nuno Tristão's along the African coast in 1441. To understand a caravel's qualities it must be compared with other sailing ships of the time. The galley, which carried both sail and rowers, required too many men in the rowing crew to be long out from land. It was capable of weathering rough seas, but the food and water problem prevented it from being used in exploration. The *nau,* a one-masted sailing vessel, could carry ample provisions but was too slow and awkward for long voyages in windy seas. The *barcha* (which was not the same as the *barca* — a smaller boat for use in rivers and harbors) and the *barinel* (or *varinel*) were vessels of some 25 tons and slightly upward, using sails primarily but also oars at times, without a deck or at best with a small covered area. They could survive the rough Atlantic, but their small size precluded long voyages away from the coast. Nevertheless, they were Henry's exploring ships to 1441 and were in use a century later.

The caravel which became the ship of exploration for three centuries was developed *after* the explorations began. In its early form it was about 75 feet long and one-third as wide. It had space without the bulkiness of the *nau,* carried two or three masts with lateen sails (later it was also square-rigged), and required but a small crew in comparison with the galley. As it could sail closer to the wind than other vessels of its size, it was more useful in long voyages and explorations. Morison credits its invention to the Portuguese and to the Spaniards of the adjacent coast around Palos, the port from which Columbus sailed.

Still another vessel developed along the Cantabrian coast had a considerable influence on deep-sea sailing — this was the *coque* or *coca.* Capable of sailing the roughest seas, it was used both for fishing and commerce. It was, of course, known to the Portuguese shipbuilders and might have influenced their ideas on design. See Morison, *Admiral of the Ocean Sea,* I, xxi-xliii; Magalhães Godinho, *Grandes découvertes,* pp. 22 ff.; Peres, *Descobrimentos portugueses,* pp. 116-127; Peres (ed.), *História Portugal Monumental,* III, 609-624.

5 *Quadro elementar,* I, 292-294, XIV, 164-166; Silva Marques, *Descobrimentos,* I, doc. 224. In 1414 the Council of Lisbon informed the King that because of the high prices of cereals in Moslem lands at that time many ships which customarily sailed to France, England, and Flanders were carrying cereals to Africa, causing a shortage in Portugal. They asked for a prohibition on cereal export, which the King granted, adding chestnuts, almonds, nuts, and other foods as well as variety of arms, steel, and iron. He probably did this as one of his preparations for the coming attack on Ceuta. These products are largely the same prohibited in many church councils, though in fact such trade was usually carried on and both export and import taxes were levied on exports to and imports from Moslem territories. Azurara states that the most common gold coin in Portugal was the *valedia,* a Moslem coin, because of the exports from Algarve to Africa. Such trade had long been customary, he says, during the reigns of former kings. See Gama Barros, *Administração pública,* IX, 63, X, 317-325.

6 The reader may want to know more about the art of navigation which carried the Portuguese over the high seas, but as this was a development that came primarily after 1415, its discussion lies beyond the scope of this book. Prior to the Atlantic discoveries, navigation was largely confined to the Mediterranean and to the Atlantic coast of Europe. Distances were not great and there were many landmarks to keep a captain on his route.

Vessels that got out of sight of land in the Atlantic ran many dangers, and historians are still bitterly disputing over the "evidence" about such ships that, having been blown off course, made discoveries of new lands during the fifteenth century or even prior to that time. Nationalistic bias has contributed much heat but little light to the clarification of many aspects of exploration.

Before Henry the Navigator's time, even to the time of Columbus, navigational instruments were simple and needed be only relatively simple. Morison remarks apropos of the art of navigation: "Our age is so filled with inventions that Columbus's great discovery is often credited to some recently invented gadget such as the astrolabe. . . . But the only instrument indispensable for Columbus was the mariner's compass, which reached the form that he used in the thirteenth century." See Morison, *Admiral of the Ocean Sea,* I, xxxiv-xxxv; A Fontura da Costa, *A marinharia dos descobrimentos* (Lisbon, 1934), and *Ciência náutica portuguesa,* in *Mundo português,* III, 539-577, with a bibliography on navigation.

BRIEF-TITLE BIBLIOGRAPHY
See chapter and note for fuller information

Almeida, *História de Portugal* ....I, 1
Almeida, *História da Igreja* ....II, 12
Altamira, *Historia de España* ....III, 1
Amari, *Nuovi ricordi arabici* ....VI, 1
Aragão, *Moedas de Portugal* ....V, 6
Archivo Histórico Portuguez ....II, 4
Azevedo, J. Lucio de, *Épocas de Portugal económico* ....IX, 1
Azevedo, Pedro de, *Porto franco de Caminha* ....IV, 1
Baião, *História da expansão portuguesa* ....I, 2
Ballesteros y Beretta, *Sevilla* ....IV, 10
Belgrano, *Documenti dei Pessagno* ....VI, 6
Benjamin de Tudela, *Itinerary* ....III, 3
Bertrand, *Histoire d'Espagne* ....I, 9
Blanchard, *Documents sur Marseilles* ....III, 7
Boudin, *Histoire de Marseilles* ....III, 7
Braamcamp Freire, *Feitoria de Flandres* ....II, 4
Brandão, *Monarchia lusitana* ....II, 15
British Museum, Letters of Privilege ....VI, 11
Brito, *Monarchia lusitana* ....II, 15
Bruyssel, *Histoire commerce belgique* ....II, 4
Busquet, *Commerce de Marseilles* ....III, 7
Byrne, *Genoese shipping* ....VI, 2
Caetano, "Administração Lisboa" ....IV, 3
Canale, *Antichi navigatori genovesi* ....III, 1
Canali, *Istoria di Genova* ....III, 1
Cantineau, *Flandre-Portugal* ....I, 16
Carte, *Rolles Gascons* ....V, 5
Castro, *A formação de Portugal* ....II, 2
Cauchie, *Source de l'histoire belgique* ....VI, 3
Colmeiro, *Historia economia en España* ....I, 7
Congresso do mundo português ....I, 3
Cortesão, see Montalvor, *Régimen republicano* ....I, 9
Cortesão, "Teoria dos descobrimentos" ....VI, 15
Costa Lobo, *História da sociedade em Portugal* ....II, 8
David, *Conquest of Lisbon* ....II, 15
David, *Narratio de itinere navali* ....III, 6
D'Aussey, *Fabliaux* ....IV, 2
De expugnatione lyxbonense ....II, 15
De expugnatione scalabis ....II, 15
De Vausse, "Croisades bourguignonnes" ....II, 1
Documentos do Arquivo de Lisboa ....V, 8
                                                                        VII, 1
Doehaerd, *Gênes-Belgique* ....II, 17
Dozy, *Histoire des musulmans* ....I, 14

Dozy, *Recherches* ....I, 15
Erdman, O papado e Portugal......................................II, 12
Fabre, *Histoire de Marseilles*....................................III, 7
Francisque-Michel. *See* Michel
Finot, *Flandre-Gênes* ....II, 6
Finot, *Flandre-Espagne* ....II, 6
Finot, *France-Flandre* ....II, 6
Flórez, *España sagrada*...I, 14
Fontura da Costa, *Ciência náutica portuguesa*......................IX, 6
Fontura da Costa, *A marinharia dos descobrimentos*................IX, 6
Gama Barros, *História da administração pública*.....................II, 5
Gazzera, *Narratio de itinere navali*................................III, 7
Germain, *Histoire du commerce de Montpellier*....................III, 7
Godin, *Princes et princesses . . . de Portugal*......................III, 5
Gonçalves Pereira, *Relations economiques*...........................II, 2
Goris, *Colonie marchandes méridionales à Anvers*...................VII, 11
Heaton, *Economic history of Europe*................................I, 11
Herculano, *História de Portugal*....................................II, 13
Herculano, *Opúsculos* ....II, 2
Heyd, *Commerce du Levant*...II, 17
Historia compostellana ....II, 10
Hoys, *Marchands flamands*..VI, 2
Iria, *Descobrimentos* ....V, 4
Jourdain, *Marine militaire*...V, 7
Kervyn de Lettenhove, *Chronique Belgique*.........................II, 4
Kervyn de Lettenhove, *Histoire de la Flandre*......................II, 4
Krueger, "Genoese trade"..III, 1
La Roncière, *La découverte de l'Afrique*...........................VI, 13
La Roncière, *Marine française*.......................................I, 14
Lencastre, *Portagens e alfandegas*..................................IV, 10
Levasseur, *Commerce de la France*..................................I, 7
Leví-Provençal, *Civilisation arabe en Espagne*......................I, 9
Livermore, "Privileges of an Englishman"............................VI, 11
Lopes, *Crónica de Fernando* ....VII, 6
Lopes, *Crónica de João I*..VIII, 1
Lopez, Robert, "European merchants"...............................VI, 1
Lopez, "Genova 1253"...VI, 2
Lopez, "Majorcans and Genoese".....................................VI, 2
Lopez, *Genova marinara* ....II, 10
Lopez, *Storia delle colonie genovesi*...............................VI, 3
Magalhães Godinho, *Grandes découvertes*...........................II, 10
Mas Latrie, *Commerce Moyen Âge*..................................III, 2
Mattoso, *História de Portugal*.......................................I, 10
Mendes Corrêa, *Raizes de Portugal*.................................II, 2
Menéndez Pidal, *España del Cid*.....................................II, 2
Meyer, *Annales flandricarum* ....II, 4
Michel, *Commerce de Bordeaux*......................................IV, 8
Michel, *Portugais-Français* ....II, 9
Montalvor, *Régimen republicano*......................................I, 9
Morison, *Admiral of the Ocean Sea*..................................IX, 4

Narratio de itinere navali...III, 6
Oliveira, Eduardo Freire de, *Elementos história Lisboa*..............IV, 10
Oliveira, Miguel de, *Ordem de Cister*...............................II, 12
Peragallo, *Colonia italiana*..VI, 2
Peres, *Como nasceu Portugal*..II, 2
Peres, *Descobrimentos portugueses*..................................VI, 13
Peres, *História de Portugal*..I, 2
Perez Embid, *La rivalidad castellana-portuguesa*....................VI, 13
Pessanha, *Os almirantes Pessanhas*..................................VI, 6
Pessanha, *Noticia dos almirantes Pessanhas*.........................VI, 9
Pinchart, *Commerce Gelges-Vénetiens*................................VI, 4
Pirenne, *Bibliographie belgique* ....II, 4
Pirenne, *Histoire de Belgique*......................................II, 4
Pirenne, *Histoire de l'Europe*......................................I, 9
Pirenne, *Medieval Cities*...I, 9
Po, *Marina italiana*..II, 10
Postan and Rich, *Cambridge Economic History*........................I, 11
Portugaliae monumenta histórica....................................I, 15
Prestage, *Portuguese Pioneers*......................................I, 1
Rau, *Exploração do sal de Setúbal*..................................III, 9
Rau, *Feiras medievais portuguesas*..................................II, 4
Reatz, *Seeversicherungsrechts* ....VII, 9
Rebello da Silva, and Santarém, *Quadro elementar*...................II, 15
Recueil des ordonnances des rois de France.........................V, 5
Reiffenberg, *Belgique-Portugal* ....III, 7
Revista portuguesa de história.....................................V, 11
Rogers, *Vivaldi Expedition*...VI, 3
Ruddock, *Italian Merchants in Southampton*..........................VI, 2
Russell, *Galés portuguesas*...VIII, 2
Russell, *English Intervention in Spain and Portugal*................VII, 5
Rymer, *Foedera . . . reges angliae*.................................IV, 1
Saavedra Machado, "Os ingleses em Portugal"..........................I, 4
Saavedra Machado, "Expedições normandas"............................I, 14
Sampaio, *Estudos históricos e económicos*...........................II, 6
Santarém, and Rebello da Silva, *Quadro elementar*...................II, 15
Shillington and Chapman, *England-Portugal*..........................IV, 1
Silva Marques, *Descobrimentos*......................................IV, 5
Suarez Fernandez, "El Atlántico y el Mediterraneo"...................VIII, 1
Thieury, *Portugal-Normandie* ....I, 7
Tovar, *Portugal e Veneza*...VI, 5
Tudela, Rabbi Benjamin, *Itinerary*..................................III, 3
Vandenbussche, *Flandre-Portugal* ....I, 13
Varenbergh, *Pays-Bas-Portugal* ....V, 12
Veiga Simões, *Flandre-Portugal*.....................................II, 16
Verlinden, *Expansion du Portugal*...................................V, 11
Verlinden, *Le problème de l'expansion*..............................VIII, 3
Vimaranis monumenta histórica......................................I, 15
Viterbo, *Elucidário* ....I, 15
Warnkoenig, *Histoire de la Flandre*.................................II, 4

INDEX

For names of authors and works cited,
see Brief-Title Bibliography, 113–115.

A

Abbeville, 35, 48
Afonso II, 32
Afonso III, 34-38 *passim*
Afonso IV, 56, 58-61 *passim*
Afonso Henriques, 11, 15-18, 21-22;
  Papacy and, 24-25, 32-33
Africa, North: João's invasion of
  Ceuta, 1-2, 82-90 *passim;* trade
  with, 5, 20, 21-22, 30, 36, 42, 43,
  53, 62, 64; Vandals in, 3
Africa, Northwest, 49, 58-59, 106 n.
  13
Agriculture, 5, 39, 61, 83
Aimeric d'Ebrard, 34, 38
Alans, 3
Albert, Duke of Holland, 76
Albufeira, 15
Alcacer do Sal, attacks on, 12, 19,
  21, 22, 27, 32
Alcaide, 30, 34, 37
Alcaide do mar, 37
Alcobaça, 13, 27, 32
Além mar, 36, 44
Alexandria, 5
Alfeizarão, 13
Alfonso of Aragón, 12
Alfonso VI of Castile, 9-11
Alfonso VII of Castile, 16, 21
Alfonso X of Castile, 34, 38
Algarve (El-Gharb), 22, 24, 40, 42,
  51, 97 n. 3, 101 n. 4
Aljubarrota, 74, 85
Almada, 22, 27
Almería, 51
Almirante-mor, 54
Almocreves (muleteers), 30
Alvôr, 15, 26
Amadeo II, Count of Savoy, 17
Amalfi, 20
Amiens, 78
Andalucia, 35, 36, 58
Andeiro, João Fernandes, 63, 71, 73
Apulia, Normans in, 8
Aquitaine, 25, 33, 42-44
Aragon, 4, 52, 56; Portugal's rela-
  tions with, 24, 65, 89; war against
  Moslems, 59

Asturias, 4
Atlantic exploration, 57 *(map)*, 58-
  59, 64, 83, 104 n. 8, 105 n. 13, 112
  n. 6
Atouguia, 13
Aveiro, 13
Ave, river, 13
Azores, 2, 58
Azurara, 13, 84, 85, 88, 110 n. 1,
  112 n. 5

B

Baixel, 36
Balearic Islands, 21, 49, 53, 81
Bapaume, 29-30
Barca, 36, 92 n. 13, 111 n. 4
Barcelona, 24
Barcha, 88, 111 n. 4
Barco, 36
Barcos saveiros, 36
Bardi family, 56
Barinel, 88, 111 n. 4
Bayonne, 44
Beatrice, daughter of Alfonso X, 34
Beatriz, daughter of Fernando, 63,
  71-72, 73
Beatriz, daughter of João I, 80
Benimerines, 59
Benjamin de Tudela, 97 n. 3
Bethencourt, Jean de, 87
Biscay, 52, 65, 81, 88
Bologna, 38
Bolsa, 44, 69, 102 n. 6
Bona, 20
Bordeaux, 33, 52
Bornstaple, 64
Bougia, 21, 22, 62
Boulogne, 48
Braga, 16, 25, 73
Bristol, 64
Britain, 3. *See also* England
Brittany, 44-45, 79, 88
Bruges: fairs in, 12, 29, 47; trade
  with, 40, 52, 76, 81, 100 n. 2
Burgundy, 8, 28
Byzantine Empire, 20, 21

C

Cádiz, 51, 53
Cahorsins, 56, 62, 66
Calatrava, religious order, 39
Cambridge, Earl of, 71
Caminha, 13, 78
Camões, Luis, 78-79
Canale, Michele, 50
Canary Islands, 58-59, 86, 87, 106 n. 4
Cantabria, 111 n. 4
Cape Bojador, 2
Cape of Good Hope, 2
Cape St. Vincent, 2
Cape Verdi Islands, 2
Caravel, sailing vessel, 6, 36, 88, 104
    n. 8, 111 n. 4
Carib, 6, 95 n. 10, 111 n. 4
Carissimus mercator noster, 52, 54
Carregador (wharfinger), 62
Carta mercatoria, 46
Carta de segurança, 77
Carthaginians, 3
Castile, 4, 9; England and, 45, 75;
    France and, 45, 62; Portugal and,
    15-16, 24, 25, 36, 63, 64, 71, 77-78,
    86, 87, 89, 108 n. 1; trade in, 56;
    war against Moslems, 59
Castro, Inez de, 61, 73
Castro Marim, 39
Catalonia, 4, 21; Catalans, in foreign
    countries, 30, 51, 52, 62, 65, 86
Cávado, river, 13
Ceuta, João I's capture of, 1-2, 82-90
    passim; trade with, 22, 33, 50, 51,
    91 n. 1
Champagne, fairs of, 12, 41, 47, 54
Charlemagne, 5
Charles V of France, 62
Charters, 56, 62, 74, 77, 78, 83, 105 n.
    11
Chartres, 35
Chichester, 64
China, trade with, 5
Christianity, attitude of Vikings to-
    ward, 7-8; Moslems and, 1-19 pas-
    sim, 22-24. See also Church; Cru-
    sades; Papacy
Chronique Rimée, 7
Church-state conflicts, 16, 32-33, 35-
    36. See also Papacy

Cistercians, 16-17, 27
Class structure, 61, 66-67, 83
Clement V, pope, 53
Clement VI, pope, 59
Cluny, monastery in, 10
Coca, 111 n. 4
Coimbra, 6, 13, 16; Côrtes of, 74, 77,
    78; University of, 38
Coina, river, 13
Columbus, Christopher, 2, 88, 90
Commerce, 5, 12, 15, 18, 38-48, 61-
    72. See also King: commercial ac-
    tivity of; Trade
Commercial classes, 61
Commines, 35
Companha, 110 n. 8
Companhia das naus, 69-70, 78, 110
    . n. 8
Compass, 112 n. 6
Condado Portucalense, 91 n. 2
Constance, wife of Alfonso VI, 10
Constance, daughter of Pedro, 65
Constantinople, 21, 51
Coque, 95 n. 10, 111 n. 4
Cornwall, 3
Corregedores, 66
Corretor, 37
Corsica, 20, 21
Côrtes, 31, 65, 66, 68, 110 n. 8. See
    also Coimbra
Crusades, 8, 12, 18, 21, 26, 28-37
    passim
Crusaders, influence in Iberian Pen-
    insula, 5, 9-19, 24, 26, 27, 96 n. 17;
    influence on trade in Mediterra-
    nean, 20, 50
Currency, 12, 22, 33, 35, 37, 44, 54,
    65

D

Dagobert I, 3
Danes, contact with Portugal, 7, 26
Dartmouth, 64
Diego Gelmirez, bishop of Compos-
    tella, 95 n. 10
Dinís, king of Portugal, reign of,
    33, 34, 38-48, 53-55, 59, 69
Douai, 29
Douro, river, 11, 13, 36
Duarte, son of João I, 1, 84-85
Dulce, daughter of Ramón Beren-
    guer IV, 24

E

Eannes Cotta, 55
Eble, Count of Rouci, 9-10
Economic revival of Europe, 11-13
Edrisi, Moslem geographer, 6, 13
Edward I of England, 43-47, 53
Edward II of England, 43, 47, 53, 54, 56
Edward III of England, 58, 59, 71
Egypt, trade with, 5, 49
Eleanor of Aquitaine, 25
El-Gharb, 49. See also Algarve
El Mehdia, 20
Elvas, 6
England, 3; Atlantic explorations and, 59; feudalism in, 9; foreign merchants in, 52, 53; Portugal and, 12, 15, 18, 24-26, 28-36 passim, 39-40, 42-46, 51, 56, 58, 60, 64, 66, 68, 70-76 passim, 78-79, 83, 88; Vikings in, 7, 8; war with France, 45. See also Aquitania
Enrique II of Castile, 71, 75
Enrique III of Castile, 87
Era of Caesar, 96 n. 15
Era of Christ, 96 n. 15
Ericeira, 13
Ervedal, river, 27
Esposende, 13
Eudes, Duke of Burgundy, 10
Eudes III, Duke of Burgundy, 25
Europe, Northern: economic revival in, 11-13; Italian trade in, 52; Portugal's relations with, 3-4, 28-36 passim, 39-49 passim, 59-60
Évora, 6, 22
Exeter, 64

F

Fairs, 12-13, 39, 94 n. 4; at Bruges, 12, 29, 47; at Champagne, 12, 41, 47, 54; at Montpellier, 24; San Demetrio, 14, 20
Fão, 13
Faro, 15, 42
Feitoria (trading post), 26, 45, 52, 75, 76, 81, 110 n. 8
Fernando I of Castile, 9, 10
Fernando IV of Castile, 46
Fernando II of León, 24
Fernando of Portugal, 61-72 passim, 104 n. 5, 110 n. 1
Fernando, son of Sancho I, 3
Fernão Lopes, 62, 63, 65, 85
Ferrara, 53
Feudalism, 9

Finot, Jules, 24
Flanders, Count of, 44, 46
Flanders, 7; England and, 68, 75-76; France and, 47-48, 68, 75-76; Italian trade with, 51, 53; Portugal and, 8, 18, 25-26, 28-36 passim, 39-40, 44-45, 66, 75, 79, 80, 81, 83, 88, 100 n. 2
Florence, 52, 56, 66, 103 n. 5
Flores de las leyes (Jacome Ruiz), 38
Foral (charter), 27, 30, 37, 68. See also Charters
Fowey, 64
Foz, 13
France, 3, 19, 51; Atlantic explorations and, 59; England and, 45; feudalism in, 9; Flanders and, 47-48, 68, 75-76; Italian merchants in, 53; Portugal and, 12, 18, 22, 25, 26, 28-36 passim, 39-40, 42-43, 55-56, 58, 60, 62, 65, 66, 68, 70, 76, 83, 88; Vikings in, 7
Freight rates, law of 1372, 66
Frisians, 26, 32
Fuenterrabia, 81

G

Gaia, 13, 35, 36, 66, 101 n. 11
Galera, 88
Galere di Fiandra, 59
Galés, 64, 75, 88, 104 n. 8, 111 n. 4
Galicia, 7, 11, 88; trade, 12, 30, 36, 81
Gama, Vasco da, 2, 88, 90
Gascony, 33, 42, 43
Genoa, 15, 20-22 passim, 33; in Atlantic explorations, 58, 86; Portugal's relations with, 49-50, 54-55, 62, 64, 65, 75, 80, 103 n. 5; rivalry between Venice and, 62
Germany, 9, 51, 52; Portugal and, 18, 26, 88
Gesta Caroli Magni, 7
Ghent, 29, 35, 76, 100 n. 2
Gibraltar, 2-3, 4, 22, 49, 51
Gilbert of Hastings, 18
Gomeira, 107 n. 4
Goris, A., 69-70
Granada, 36, 64, 69, 86-89 passim
Greece, 5, 7, 19
Gregory VII, pope, 10, 16
Guadiana, river, 39
Guglielmo Sardena, 15
Gui de Dampierre, Count, 40
Guilds, 29, 109 n. 8

Guilherme, Dean of Silves, 26, 27
Guimarães, 11
Guinea, 3

H
Hanseatic merchants, 40
Harbors, improved, 36
Harfleur, 42, 48
Henrique, son of João I, 1. *See also*
    Henry the Navigator
Henry of Burgundy, 8-11 *passim*, 21
Henry II of Castile, 64
Henry III of Castile, 87
Henry II of England, 25, 28
Henry III of England, 31-33
Henry IV of England, 79
Henry V of England, 82, 89
Henry the Navigator, 1, 39, 64, 75,
    84-85, 88-90
*Hermandad de las villas de la ma-
    rina de Castilla*, 46
Holland, Duke of, 76, 89
Holy Land, Crusades to 9, 12, 21, 32
Hospitallers, 32, 39
Hugh, Duke of Burgundy, 10
Hugh of Chalon, 10
Hugh, Abbot of Cluny, 10, 94 n. 2
Hundred Years' War, 58, 65, 75

I
Iberian Peninsula, Reconquest of,
    9-19, 21. *See also* Portugal; Spain;
    and specific cities
Ibn al Koutia, 7
India, 2, 5, 58
Innocent II, pope, 15
Insurance, maritime, 44, 69-70
Isabella the Catholic, 75
Islam. *See* Moslems
Italy: in Atlantic explorations, 58,
    59, 104 n. 8; commercial develop-
    ment of, 50-53 *passim;* effect of
    lack of unified kingdom on trade,
    45; foreign trade, 19, 20, 21, 41,
    50-53, 78-80; maritime laws, 70;
    Normans, in, 10; Portugal's rela-
    tions with, 5, 17, 22, 39-40, 49-60
    passim, 62, 83; skill of seamen, 54-
    55. *See also* specific cities

J
Jacome Ruiz, 38
Jaime II of Aragon, 86
Jakobsland, 7
Jean II of France, 60, 62
Jeanne of Constantinople, 31

Jews in Spain and Portugal, 5,
    22, 33, 109 n. 8
João I (Grand Master of Aviz), 61,
    64; campaign in Africa, 1, 83-89
    passim; reign of, 69, 73-82, 108 n.
    1, 110 n. 1
João de Mina, 36-37
João Peculiar, bishop of Braga, 16,
    17
João das Regras, 74
John XXII, pope, 39
John, king of England, 29, 30-31
John of Gaunt, 65, 71, 74, 75
John the Fearless, Duke of Bur-
    gundy, 81
Joint stock company, 110 n. 8
Juan I of Castile, 71, 72, 73
Juan II of Castile, 85, 108 n. 1

K
King: commercial activity of, 30,
    33-36, 41-42, 56, 61-72 *passim*, 80;
    title bestowed on Afonso Hen-
    riques, 15-16, 24-25
Knights Templar, 32, 39

L
Lagos, 15, 40, 42, 44
Lancelotto Malocello, 58
Lançarote da Franca, 106 n. 4
La Rochelle, 44, 46, 48, 50, 51
La Salle, Gadifer de, 87
Laudomanes, 93 n. 15
Leça, 13
Legistas (men of law), 38, 66
Leiria, 39, 66
Le Landit, 3, 92 n. 7
Leo IX, pope, 8
León, 4, 9; political rivalry between
    Portugal and, 15-16, 24, 25
Leonor, daughter of Henry II, 64
Leonore of Portugal, 60
Letrados (men of letters), 38, 66
Levant, 2, 4, 5, 13, 19, 20
"Liberties" (exemptions), 56
Libro del Conoscimiento, 105 n. 13
Lille, 19, 35, 100 n. 2
Lima, river, 13
Limoges, 30, 100 n. 2
Lisbon, 6, 7, 71, 73; bishop of, 32;
    Câmara of, 46; *Côrtes* of, 66; Cru-
    saders in, 12, 26; as port, 42, 84;
    privileges in, 30; in Reconquest,
    12, 17-18, 22; shipbuilding in, 33-
    34, 69; trade in, 30, 45, 53, 60, 65-
    66, 81, 108 n. 1, 110 n. 8

Lisbon, University of, 38
"Lissibon" (Lisbon), 7
Literature, 34, 38-39
Liz, river, 13
Lombardy, 4, 51, 52, 65
London, Portugal and, 35, 64, 74
London Corporation, 42, 46
Louis VI of France, 12
Louis IX (Saint Louis) of France, 34
Louis X of France, 54
Loulé, 15
Lourinhã, 13
Luis of Castile, 59
Lusíadas (Camões), 78-79
Lynn, 64

M

Madeira Islands, 2, 58
Madjous, 7
Malaga, 51
Malagueta, 57
Mallorca: in Atlantic explorations, 58, 86; trade with, 51, 52, 56, 62, 65
Mandeville, Sir John, 106 n. 13
Maravedi, 22
Maritime commerce, 42-48
Markets. *See* Fairs
Marseilles, 21, 26, 50, 97 n. 3, 98 n. 7
Massarelos, 13
Mathilde, Countess of Clermont, 34
Matilde of Savoy, 17
Matozinhos, 13
Mediterranean Sea: Crusades and, 12; trade in, 20, 50-54, 80-81, 109 n. 6
Mercadores alfaqueques, 22-23
Merchant class, importance of, 73-75
Merchants: compact, 44-45; difficulties of, 42-46, 59-60, 77-82 *passim;* difficulties caused by, 62-63; privileges to, 12-13, 56, 78, 82; safe-conducts for, 31, 32, 46, 47, 76. *See also* Trade
Middelbourg, 76, 81
Middle class, growth of, 66-67
Milan, 56, 62, 65
Minho, river, 11, 13, 81
Mira, 13
Mondego, river, 13, 24
Money, 87-88. *See also* Currency
Montpellier, 24, 26, 35, 97 n. 3, 98 n. 7; Portuguese students in, 38; trade agreements in, 50
Morocco, 4, 21, 22, 49-50

Moslems: invasion and conquest of Spain and Portugal, 4-6, 50; Italian cities and, 20, 21, 49, 51; Reconquest of Iberian Peninsula from, 9-19, 21-22, 26, 27, 34, 37, 58, 59, 86, 87; trade, 21-22, 24, 30, 33, 40, 55, 62, 64
Mozarabic Christians, 5-6, 10, 16, 18
Muluya, river, 86

N

Nationalism, 83, 90
Naus, 64, 88
Nave, 36
Navigation, art of, 112 n. 6
Nicolau, bishop of Silves, 26
Nobility in business, 41-42, 61-70 *passim*
Normandy, 7, 8, 52
Normans (Vikings), 6-8, 12, 92 nn. 11, 13, 93 nn. 14, 16; in Italy, 10, 20, 21; in Portugal, 15
North Sea-Mediterranean trade, 50-54 *passim,* 81
Norway, Portugal and, 80
Nossa Senhora a Franca, 107 n. 4

O

Odemira, 15
Oporto: bishop of, 33, 35-36; Charter to, 81; *Concelho* of, 55; *Córtes* of, 66; merchants of, 60, 108 n. 1, 110 n. 8; as seaport, 13, 42, 62, 84, 101 n. 11; shipbuilding in, 69
Order of Christ, 39, 55, 59
Ourique, battle of, 15

P

Palermo, 20
Palmela, 27
Pamplona, 31, 100 n. 2
Papacy: influence in Spain; Portugal's relations with, 16-17, 24-25, 55
Papacy in Avignon, 47
Paredes, 13
Paris, 32, 38, 78
Peçanha (Pessagno), Lançerote, 53, 62, 64, 65, 104 nn. 5, 6, 107 n. 4
Peçanha (Pessagno), Manuel, 48, 49, 53, 54-55, 62, 104 nn. 5, 6
Pedro the Cruel of Castile, 65
Pedro I of Portugal, 61-63, 73, 110 n. 1

Pedro, son of João I, 1, 84-85
Perdeneira, 13
Pereira, Gonçalo, 55
Pessagno, Antonio, 53
Pessagno, Manuele. *See* Peçanha, Lançerote
Pessagno. Manuele. *See* Peçanha, Manuel
Philip II, Augustus, of France, 28-29, 99 n. 2
Philip IV of France, 39, 42, 45, 47-48, 52, 102 n. 11
Philip VI of France, 58, 59
Philip II of Spain, 75
Philip of Alsace, Count of Flanders, 25
Philip the Bold, 76
Philippa of Lancaster, 75, 79, 89
Phoenicians, 2-3
Piacenzans, 56, 62, 66, 75
Pinácia, 36
Pinidelo, 13
Piracy, 6-7, 8, 31, 42, 43, 47
Pisa, 20, 21
Plymouth, 64
Poland, 88
Ponte de Lima, 12
Portimão, 15
"Portingal" (Portugal), 7
Portolanos, 13
Portugal: exports, 4-11, 12, 15, 46-47, 61; foreigners in, 8, 15, 18-19, 75, 77, 84, 85; imports, 34-35, 36, 79; map, 14; maritime growth, 26; national church, 16; national feeling, 66-67; Reconquest, 9-19, 26, 50; revenues under Fernando, 70; Royal fleet, 37, 55, 69; sailors, 33-34, 54-55; territorial expansion, 15, 86-87
Pretor of marinheiros (seamen), 33-34
Prices, 34-35, 81
Privileges, 30, 35-36, 56, 58, 60, 62, 64, 67-69, 75-84 *passim*, 102 n. 11
Products, exports and imports, 3, 5, 24, 30, 31, 33, 35, 50, 61, 77
Provençal poetry, 34, 38-39
Provence, 4, 29
Pustura, 44, 102 n. 6, 110 n. 8

R

Ramón Berenguer IV of Barcelona, 24

Raymond of Burgundy, 10, 11, 13
Religious orders, 39
Richard II of England, 71, 74, 75, 79
Richard the Lion-Hearted, 28
Robert, Count of Jerusalem, 12
Robert, Seigneur de Ghistelles, 40
Robert of Frison, 9
Robert Guiscard, 8, 10
Roger of Sicily, 8
Roman law, influence in Portugal, 38
Rouen, 35, 48
Royan, 33

S

Sacavém, river, 13
Sado, river, 12, 15, 17
Safe-conducts, 31, 32, 46, 47, 76, 102 n. 5
Safi, 51, 58
Sagas, Viking, 7
Saint Denis, 12
Saint Omer, 35
Salado, battle of, 58
Salamanca, 38
Salé (or Saleh), 22
Salvage, laws of, 31
Sancho I, 24, 26, 27, 29
Sancho II, 32-33
Sancho IV of Castile, 86
Sancho Ramírez of Aragón, 10
San Demetrius, 19, 20
San Domingos monastery, 81
San Francisco, chapel in Seville, 34
Santerém, 6, 13-14, 17, 27, 30
Santiago, 15, 25, 30
Santiago, religious order, 39
Santiago de Compostela, 7, 12
São Martinho, 13
Saracens, 9, 37. *See also* Moslems
Saragossa, 30, 100 n. 2
Sardinia, 20, 21
Scheldt, lowlands of, 28
Segovia, 35
Seine, river, 12
Selir, 13
Sesimbra, 27
Setúbal, 42
Sevilla, 34, 42, 51
Shipbuilding: by Italians, 52, 95 n. 10; in Portugal, 6, 13, 36-37, 39, 55, 68-69, 81, 92 n. 13
Shipping, 36-37
Ships, types of, 6, 36, 64, 75, 88, 104 n. 8, 111 n. 4

Shipyards *(taracenas)*, 33-34
Sicily, 20, 52, 56
Sienna, 52
Siete partidas, 38
Sigurd, king of Norway, 12
Silves, 6, 15, 26, 27
Sines, 15
Sintra, 12
Sluys, battle of, 58
Smith, Adam, 90
Social structure, 66-67, 74-75
Soria, Convention of, 86
Southampton, 64
Spain, Moslem conquest of, 4-6;
    Portugal's relations with, 11, 38,
    42-46 *passim*, 83, 85; products of,
    41-42; Reconquest from Moslems,
    9-19 *passim*, 21, 50; trade with
    foreign merchants, 19, 22, 53. *See
    also* Castile
Spice Islands, trade with, 5
State-Church struggle, 32-33, 35-36
Syria, trade with, 5, 49

T

Tagus, river, 7, 12, 13, 18, 27, 42
Tancred of Hauteville, 8
Tarik, 4
Tavira, 40
Taxes, 18, 27, 36, 37, 49
Teles, Leonor, 63, 64, 72, 73
Teresa, daughter of Afonso Hen-
    riques, 25, 28, 35
Teresa, daughter of Alfonso VI, 11
Terra Portucalense, 11, 21
Tetuán, 87, 111 n. 3
Thessalonica, 19, 20
Thibaud de Semur, 9-10
Thomas, Count of Arundel, 80
Toledo, 3, 16, 25, 30, 35, 100 n. 2
Tortosa, 21
Tournois, 35
Tours, 4
Trade, 5, 6-7, 18-19, 21, 61-72 *passim*,
    96 n. 17. *See also* specific countries
    and cities
Trade routes, map of, 23

Treaties: *1308*, 64; *1353*, 60, 64; *1386*,
    75; *1411*, 81, 84
Tunis, 20, 37, 50
Tuy, 13

U

Ulf the Galician, 8
University of Coimbra (Lisbon), 38
Urraca, daughter of Afonso Hen-
    riques, 24
Urraca, daughter of Alfonso VI, 11,
    12

V

Valença, 13
Valenciennes, 35
Varinel, 111 n. 4
Vasco da Gama, 2, 88, 90
Venice, 20, 50, 51, 52, 53, 65-66, 78,
    103 n. 5
Viana, 13, 37
Victor III, pope, 20
Vikings. *See* Normans
Vila do Conde, 13, 36
Vila dos Francos (Azambuja), 27
Vila Nova de Gaia, 35
Villanes, 15
Visigoths, 3, 4
Vivaldi brothers, 58, 86
Vouga, river, 13

W

Walcheren Island, 76
Weymouth, 64
William, Count of Holland, 82
William, Duke of Aquitania, 10
William the Conqueror, 8

Y

Yacub Almançor, 27
Ypres, 29, 35, 76

Z

Zaccaria brothers (Beneditto and
    Nicolo), 51, 52
Zeeland, 76

ACKNOWLEDGMENTS

The quality of a book, I believe, is in direct ratio to the ability of the author to profit from the advice of those who helped him. This book would no doubt be much better if I could have comprehended and included the many good suggestions given me by those abler than I to write it. The problem of the author is to know where to begin listing his debts.

However long my list of acknowledgments, and however effusive, the full extent of the debts would not be adequately revealed. First, to the libraries and archives in general. I am of the opinion that a great forward step would be taken in education if all universities were grouped around the library rather than the football stadium, but that is no doubt an unjustified personal prejudice. In the ten years that have elapsed since I first started this book and contingent studies, I cannot remember a single instance when a library or archive failed to fulfill my request; and discourtesies there were none. Although peninsular libraries are not usually so well organized as some others, what they may lack in technical efficiency they often make up in kindness.

The materials I have used have been drawn in part from my own library at the City College of New York, to the librarians of which I owe a debt I hope they never try to collect. I also drew material from Columbia University until the library was closed to those outside its staff. The New York Public Library is, of course, excellent for both material and service. Among others that may be cited are the Library of Congress, the British Museum, the Bibliothèque Nationale in Paris, the archives in Montpellier and Nimes, France, and the Biblioteca Nacional in Madrid. I have twice visited the archives of Aragon in Barcelona but none of the material herein used is drawn directly from that source.

In Italy I have used the archives in both Genoa and Venice, the Biblioteca Ambrosiana in Milan, the Biblioteca Nationale in Florence, and both the Corsiniana and Angelica in Rome.

My principal materials have been drawn, naturally, from Portugal. The Biblioteca Nacional in Lisbon is the greatest single repository of works on Portuguese history. The Director and the personnel were invariably courteous and helpful. In both the Arquivo Nacional da Torre do Tombo, directed by Dr. João Martins da Silva Marques, and the Arquivo Histórico Ultramarino, directed by Dr. Alberto Iria, I was made welcome. The excellent publications of documents by these two scholars rendered the discovery of anything substantially new on this subject highly unlikely. I have repeatedly used the library of the Sociedade de Geografia of Lisbon where their materials were courteously made available. Also, in the Biblioteca da Ajuda in Lisbon the Director, Dr. Frederico Guilherme Gavazzo Perry Vidal, was most cordial and helpful. The same is true of Dr. Manual Granada Vidal of the Biblioteca Pública Municipal of Santarém, which houses the former library of Braamcamp Freire. Conversations with Dr. José Formasinho, Historian of Lagos, were very useful to me.

In the library of the University of Coimbra I received every attention from the Director, Professor Manuel Lopes d'Almeida, and the Chief Librarian, Dr. César Pegado. Also, Mr. José Maria dos Santos gave me valuable aid in photography. In the Gabinete de Historia of Oporto the Director, Dr. J. A. Pinto Ferreira, and the Chief Paleographer, Dr. Fernando Guimarães, aided me greatly.

All the above will comprehend and forgive, however, if I say that it is to the Biblioteca Pública Municipal do Pôrto that my heart goes out. The Director, Dr. António Cruz, and the Sub-Director, Dr. Fulgencio Lopes da Silva, placed "all facilities" at my disposal, and really meant it. Nowhere else could I have worked with so much ease and so much attention. All who know "Dom Fulgencio" will say that there was never another like him. The Oporto library became and remains a real home to me.

The University of Miami Library in Coral Gables, Florida, was kind enough to provide me with a quiet corner with a wide table and bookshelves where I could install my filing case and reference books in an atmosphere of hospitality. There in a warm climate and among warmhearted people a large part of this work was written.

Readers who are averse to sentiment can stop reading here, for I want to make a number of personal acknowledgments. Suggestions from Professor Charles Boxer of King's College, London, spurred my ideas. Conversations with Professor Hernani Cidade of the University of Lisbon, and with Professor Damião Peres, as well as the many publications of both these gentlemen, were most useful. Professor Robert S. Lopez of Yale University was good enough to read some preliminary pages of this work and to offer suggestions of great value. He also gave me useful bibliographical aid and indispensable introductions to Italian archives. Professor Charles Verlinden of the University of Brussels both in person and in correspondence helped me greatly. The numerous works of both these gentlemen are cited above. For Professor Virginia Rau of the University of Lisbon no words, even of Camões, could come remotely close to expressing my gratitude. In the midst of her mountainous production of matchless works she finds time to be a true friend of visiting scholars.

I cannot end my list here. Miss Elaine Sanceau, author of many excellent works on Portugal, and Dr. A. de Magalhães Basto, erudite scholar and gentleman, both stimulated me with their conversation. Dr. Max Lieberman, now resident in France, was the source of many valuable ideas.

My friend and colleague, Professor Michael Kraus, was heroic to the point of valor, reading the entire manuscript. To him the reader owes a debt for many phrases more felicitous than I could have devised. Mrs. Sylvia Primus read the typescript and aided me in reaserch.

There are others whose friendship served me as an inspiration. Among them I would name Mrs. Maria Mendes Leal of Lisbon; Mr. Edgar Ennor of Oporto; Frederick and Denise Sacksteder of Madrid and Lisbon, friends since my university days in Madrid; Tom and Muriel Mawston of Foz do Douro; Mr. and Mrs. A. Pacheco de Carvalho of Lisbon; and finally in this personal list, D. Violeta Thadeu of Lisbon. For her aid in the search for books and to her friendship I am more endebted than I can say.

As the unsentimental readers have long since dropped off, I wish to add one more tribute — to the Pensão Mary Castro in Foz do Douro. Since 1931 the Mary Castro has been my home from time to time, and to its owner Senhor Gomes and his family, and to the *criadas* who so faithfully served me, I can only say that I command no adequate words of thanks.

The American Philosophical Society and the Social Science Research Council gave me assistance that enabled me to make three research trips to Europe. I am grateful.

A NOTE ABOUT THE AUTHOR

A native Texan, BAILEY W. DIFFIE received his B.A. from Southeastern Teachers College (1923) and his M.A. from Texas Christian University (1926), and became a Doctor en Filosofîa y Letras, Sobresaliente, in Madrid, Spain, in 1929. He joined the faculty of the City College, New York, as an instructor in 1930 and has served on it up until the present time, becoming a full professor in 1951. He has been a Rockefeller Foundation Fellow (1940–1941), Visiting Lecturer at both Cornell and Yale Universities (1943, 1946–1947), has twice been elected to the editorial board of *Hispanic American Historical Review,* and was elected a member of the general committee of the Conference on Latin-American History, serving as chairman in 1954.

Professor Diffie's research for PRELUDE TO EMPIRE began in 1948 in Portugal, and was carried on 1948–1949, 1952, 1957, and 1958–1959 in Portugal, Spain, France, England, Belgium, and Italy.